WRITERS ON ORGANIZATIONS

WRITERS ON ORGANIZATIONS

D.S. Pugh
D.J. Hickson
C.R. Hinings

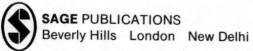

SAGE PUBLICATIONS
Beverly Hills   London   New Delhi

For information address:

SAGE Publications, Inc.
275 South Beverly Drive
Beverly Hills, California 90212

Printed in the United States of America

Library of Congress Cataloging in Publication Data

Pugh, Derek Salman.
    Writers on organizations.

    Includes index.
    1. Organization—Addresses, essays, lectures.
2. Industrial management—Addresses, essays, lectures.
I. Hickson, David John. II. Hinings, C. R. (Christopher
Robin) III. Title.
HM131.P74   1985   302.3′5   84-27666
ISBN 0-8039-2419-4
ISBN 0-8039-2444-5 (pbk.)

FIRST PRINTING

First published by Hutchinson, 1964
Subsequent U.K. publication by Penguin Books Ltd, 1971, 1973, 1975-1983

WRITERS
ON
ORGANIZATIONS

To our parents and to
our professional father-figures

Contents

Introduction to the First Edition

It is a commonplace of discussions among administrators and managers to hear that all organizations are different. Frequently the implication is that there can be little in common between them and consequently no coherent description of organizations. Even so, administrators continue to forgather to discuss their problems in a way which suggests that, after all, they find they have common interests and value each other's experience and advice.

Even if all organizations are indeed different it is possible to state these differences and to classify them, so that something useful can be said about various kinds of organizations and the ways in which they function. In this book we have presented a synopsis of the work of a number of leading writers who have attempted this analysis. These authors have a variety of different backgrounds. Some are drawing upon their experience as practising managers, some on their knowledge of local and national government administration, some on the findings of their research work. All are modern in that the influence of their work has been felt within the last fifty years. All have attempted to draw together information and distil theories of how organizations function and how they should be managed.

Their writings have been theoretical in the sense that they have tried to discover generalizations applicable to all organizations. Every act of an administrator rests on assumptions about what has happened and conjectures about what will happen; that is to say, it rests on theory. Theory and practice are inseparable.

Our object has been to give a direct exposition of the author's views. We have not essayed critical analysis which would be a quite different task. It is our hope that the reader will bring his own critical appraisal to each writer. Even so, we are extremely conscious of the very considerable selection and compression which is involved in presenting a man's work in a few pages. Some distortions must inevitably result. We can only plead the best of intentions in that our hope is to entice the reader to go to the originals in their richness and complexity.

We are grateful to J. P. Martin-Bates who, in sponsoring this volume for the Administrative Staff College, Henley-on-Thames, gave us every encouragement. Morris Brodie not only acted as the link between ourselves and the College but gave generously of constructive comment and criticism. Our colleague Tom Lupton read the manuscript and made a number of helpful suggestions. We also wish to thank Miss Mildred Wilhelm for her many hours spent in typing the manuscript and our colleagues in the Industrial Administration Research Unit for their forbearance. The arduous task of compiling the index was ably undertaken by Miss C. Brookes. Our wives, as always, suffered most in the cause.

I. A. Research Unit
Birmingham College of
Advanced Technology
1963

Note to the Second Edition

The demand for a second edition of this book has given us the opportunity of revising a considerable proportion of the essays included, and of bringing them up to date where necessary. We have also added descriptions of the work of a further nine writers on the subject. Our aim in this revision and expansion has remained the same: to present a concise introductory account of each writer's contribution in order to give a general overview of the field, and to attract the reader to follow his initial interest by going to the original sources, which as before are fully listed. Simultaneously with the publication of this edition, a companion volume, *Organizations: Selected Readings*, edited by D. S. Pugh is being issued. This brings together in convenient form extracts from the work of several of the writers summarized here.

We are grateful to the Faculty of Business Administration of the University of Alberta, and to our colleagues there, for providing the occasion of our meeting to complete this revision.

Organizational Behavior Research Unit
University of Alberta
1970

Note to the Third Edition

The continuing sales, over a period of a decade, of the second edition of this book have been most gratifying. With changing organizational issues and with new work making an impact, it is appropriate now to offer a third edition. We have added descriptions of new writers and brought others up to date, and made some rearrangement of the sections. Since it is one of the attractions of this introductory book that it should be relatively slim, we have regretfully decided that certain writers whose work is no longer the subject of debate in the field should be dropped. They have made their contribution and we salute them.

The aim of the present work is, as before, to present a concise introductory account of leading writers whose contribution is currently the subject of interest and argument and to attract the reader to go, as appropriate, to the original listed sources. A revised edition of the companion volume *Organization Theory: Selected Readings*, edited by D. S. Pugh, presents extracts from the work of many of the writers given here.

The Netherlands Institute for Advanced Study in the Humanities and Social Sciences provided us with an opportunity of meeting to complete this revision. We are grateful to them and to Helena Pugh, who compiled the index.

N.I.A.S.
Wassenaar, Holland
1982

I · *The Structure of Organizations*

The decisive reason for the advance of bureaucratic organization has always been its purely technical superiority over any other form of organization.
Max Weber

It would be entirely premature, then, to assume that bureaucracies maintain themselves solely because of their efficiency.
Alvin W. Gouldner

The danger lies in the tendency to teach the principles of administration as though they were scientific laws, when they are really little more than administrative expedients found to work well in certain circumstances but never tested in any systematic way.
Joan Woodward

The beginning of administrative wisdom is the awareness that there is no one optimum type of management system.
Tom Burns

It may not be impossible to run an effective organization of 5,000 employees non-bureaucratically, but it would be so difficult that no one tries.
The Aston Group

The effective organization has integrating devices consistent with the diversity of its environment. The more diverse the environment and the more differentiated the organization, the more elaborate the integrating devices.
Paul Lawrence and Jay Lorsch

Historically, administrators have rarely changed their daily routine and their positions of power except under the strongest pressures.
Alfred D. Chandler

The price system has advantages over central planning in circumstances where the relevant information is summarized by price signals.
Oliver E. Williamson

All organizations have to make provision for continuing activities directed towards the achievement of given aims. Regularities in activities such as task allocation, supervision and coordination are developed. Such regularities constitute the organization's structure and the fact that these activities can be arranged in various ways means that organizations can have differing structures. Indeed, in some respects every organization is unique. But many writers have examined a variety of structures to see if any general principles can be extracted. This variety, moreover, may be related to variations in such factors as the objectives of the organization, its size, ownership, geographical location and technology of manufacture, which produce the characteristic differences in structure of a bank, a hospital, a mass production factory or a local government department.

The writers in this section are concerned to identify different forms of organizational structures and to explore their implications and the factors which produce them. Max Weber outlines three different types of organization by examining the bases for wielding authority. Alvin W. Gouldner starts from one of Weber's types, bureaucracy, and shows that even in one organization three variants of this type can be found. Joan Woodward has studied the relationship between production systems, technology and structure in manufacturing concerns. She argues that the production technology is a major determinant of the structure. Tom Burns is concerned with the impact of changing technology, and the attempts of old-established firms to adjust to new situations.

Derek Pugh and the Aston Group suggest that it is more realistic to talk in terms of dimensions of structures rather than types, and Paul Lawrence and Jay Lorsch emphasize that it is the appropriateness of the organization's structure in relation to its environmental requirements which is the basis of effectiveness. Alfred Chandler shows how structure is affected by organizational strategy and Oliver Williamson analyses the factors which lead to hierarchical structures rather than market relationships.

All the contributors to this chapter suggest that an appropriate structure is vital to the efficiency of an organization and must be the subject of careful study in its own right.

Max Weber

Max Weber (1864–1920) was born in Germany. He qualified in law and then became a member of the staff of Berlin University. He remained an academic for the rest of his life, having a primary interest in the broad sweep of the historical development of civilizations through studies of the sociology of religion and the sociology of economic life. In his approach to both of these topics he showed a tremendous range in examining the major world religions such as Judaism, Christianity and Buddhism, and in tracing the pattern of economic development from pre-feudal times. These two interests were combined in his classic studies of the impact of Protestant beliefs on the development of capitalism in Western Europe and the USA. Weber had the prodigious output and ponderous style typical of German philosophers, but those of his writings which have been translated into English have established him as a major figure in sociology.

Weber's principal contribution to the study of organizations was his theory of authority structures which led him to characterize organizations in terms of the authority relations within them. This stemmed from a basic concern with why individuals obeyed commands, why people do as they are told. To deal with this problem Weber made a distinction between *power*, the ability to force people to obey, regardless of their resistance, and *authority*, where orders are voluntarily obeyed by those receiving them. Under an authority system, those in the subordinate role see the issuing of directives by those in the superordinate role as legitimate. Weber distinguished between organizational types according to the way in which authority is legitimized. He outlined three pure types which he labelled 'charismatic', 'traditional', and 'rational–legal', each of which is expressed in a particular administrative apparatus or organization. These pure types are distinctions which are useful for analysing organizations, although any real organization may be a combination of them.

The first mode of exercising authority is based on the personal qualities of the leader. Weber used the Greek term *charisma* to mean any quality of the individual's personality by virtue of which he is set apart from ordinary men and treated as endowed with supernatural, superhuman or at least specifically exceptional powers or qualities. This is the position of the prophet, messiah or political leader, whose organization consists of himself and a set of disciples: the disciples have the job of mediating between the leader and the masses. The typical case of this kind is a small-scale revolutionary movement either religious or political in form, but many organizations have had 'charismatic' founders, such as Lord Nuffield (Morris Motors) and Henry Ford. However, as the basis of authority is in the characteristics of one person and commands are based on his inspiration, this type of organization has a built-in instability. The question of succession always arises when the leader dies and the authority has to be passed on. Typically, in political and religious organizations the movement splits with the various disciples claiming to be the 'true' heirs to the charismatic leader. Thus the process is usually one of fission. The tendencies towards this kind of breakdown can be seen in the jockeying for position of Hitler's lieutenants, Himmler and Goering, during the first few months of 1945. It exemplifies the problem of an heir to the leader, and even if the leader himself nominates his successor, he will not necessarily be accepted. It is unlikely that another charismatic leader will present himself; and so the organization must lose its charismatic form, becoming one of the two remaining types. If the succession becomes hereditary, the organization becomes traditional in form; if the succession is determined by rules a bureaucratic organization develops.

The bases of order and authority in *traditional* organizations are precedent and usage. The rights and expectations of various groups are established in terms of taking what has always happened as sacred; the great arbiter in such a system is custom. The leader in such a system has authority by virtue of the status that he has inherited, and the extent of his authority is fixed by custom. When charisma is traditionalized by making its transmission hereditary, it becomes part of the role of the leader rather than being part of his personality. The actual organizational form under a traditional authority system can take one of two patterns. There is the *patrimonial* form where officials are personal servants, dependent on the leader for remuneration. Under the *feudal* form the officials have much more autonomy with their own sources of income and a traditional relationship of loyalty towards the leader. The feudal system has a material basis of tithes, fiefs and beneficiaries all resting on past usage and a system of customary rights and duties. Although Weber's examples are historical his insight is equally applicable to modern organizations. Managerial positions are often handed down from father to son as firms establish their own dynasties based on hereditary transmission. Selection and appointment may be based on kinship rather than expertise. Similarly, ways of doing things in many organizations are justified in terms of always having been done that way *as a reason in itself*, rather than on the basis of a rational analysis.

The concept of rational analysis leads to Weber's third type of authority system, the rational–legal one, with its bureaucratic organizational form. This, Weber sees as the dominant institution of modern society. The system is called rational because the means are expressly designed to achieve certain specific goals, i.e. the organization is like a well-designed machine with a certain function to perform, and every part of the machine contributes to the attainment of maximum performance of that function. It is legal because authority is exercised by means of a system of rules and procedures through the office which an individual occupies at a particular time. For such organization Weber uses the name 'bureaucracy'. In common usage, bureaucracy is synonymous with inefficiency, an emphasis on red tape, and excessive writing and recording. Specifically, it is identified with inefficient public administration. But in terms of his own definition Weber states that a bureaucratic organization is technically the most efficient form of organization possible. 'Precision, speed, unambiguity, knowledge of files, continuity, discretion, unity, strict subordination, reduction of friction and of material and personal costs – these are raised to the optimum point in the strictly bureaucratic administration.' Weber himself uses the machine analogy when he says that the bureaucracy is like a modern machine, while other organizational forms are like nonmechanical methods of production.

The reason for the efficiency of the bureaucracy lies in its organizational form. As the means used are those which will best achieve the stated ends, it is unencumbered by the personal whims of the leader or by traditional procedures which are no longer applicable. This is because bureaucracies represent the final stage in depersonalization. In such organizations there is a series of officials, each of whose roles is circumscribed by a written definition of his authority. These offices are arranged in a hierarchy, each successive step embracing all those beneath it. There is a set of rules and procedures within which every possible contingency is theoretically provided for. There is a 'bureau' for the safe keeping of all written records and files, it being an important part of the rationality of the system that information is written down. A clear separation is made between personal and business affairs, bolstered by a contractual method of appointment in terms of technical qualifications for office. In such an organization authority is based in the office and commands are obeyed because the rules state that it is within the competence of a particular office to issue such commands. Also important is the stress on the appointment of experts. One of the signs of a developing bureaucracy is the growth of professional managers and an increase in the number of specialist experts with their own departments.

For Weber this adds up to a highly efficient system of co-ordination and control. The rationality of the organization shows in its ability to 'calculate' the consequences of its action. Because of the hierarchy of authority and the system of rules, control of the actions of individuals in the organization is assured; this is the depersonalization. Because of the employment of experts who have their specific areas of responsibility and the use of files, there is an amalgamation of the best available knowledge and a record of past behaviour of the organization. This enables predictions to be made about future events. The organization has rationality: 'the methodical attainment of a definitely given and practical end by means of an increasingly precise calculation of means'.

This is where the link between Weber's interest in religion and organizations occurs. Capitalism as an economic system is based on the rational long-term calculation of economic gain. Initially for this to happen, as well as the expansion of world markets, a particular moral outlook is needed. Weber saw this as being supplied by the Protestant religion after the Reformation with its emphasis on this world and the need for individuals to show their salvation through their industry on earth. Thus, economic activity gradually became labelled as a positive good rather than as a negative evil. Capitalism was launched on its path, and this path was cleared most easily through the organizational form of bureaucracy which supplied the apparatus for putting economic rationality into practice. Providing as it does efficiency and regularity, bureaucratic administration is a necessity for any long-term economic calculation. So with increasing industrialization, bureaucracy becomes the dominant method of organizing, and so potent is it that it becomes characteristic of other areas of society such as education, government, politics, etc. Finally, the bureaucratic organization becomes typical of all the institutions of modern society.

Most studies of the formal, structural characteristics of organizations over the past two decades have started from the work of Max Weber. His importance lies in having made the first attempt to produce systematic categories for organizational analysis.

Bibliography

Weber, M., *The Protestant Ethic and the Spirit of Capitalism*, New York: Scribner's, 1930.

Weber, M., *The Theory of Social and Economic Organization*, New York: Free Press, 1947.

Gerth, H. H., and Mills, C. W. (eds.), *From Max Weber: Essays in Sociology*, New York: Galaxy, 1958.

Alvin W. Gouldner

Alvin W. Gouldner (1920–1980) was an American sociologist who held the Max Weber Chair of Social Theory at Washington University, St Louis. He conducted research into social problems for the American Jewish Committee, and worked on industrial organization, including consulting for the Standard Oil Company of New Jersey. In the last two decades of his life he was particularly concerned with the development of sociological theory and with the role of knowledge in society.

Gouldner has applied Weber's concept of bureaucracy and its functioning to modern industrial organizations. Weber's analysis was based on the assumption that the members of an organization will in fact comply with the rules and obey orders. He asked on what basis do the rule-promulgators and the order-givers obtain their legitimate authority. He gave no attention to the problem of establishing the legitimacy of authority, in the face of opposition and a refusal to consent on the part of the governed. This is a situation frequently met, for example, when a bureaucratic authority attempts to supplant a traditionalistic one, or when the rule of the expert or the rational–legal wielder of power is faced with resistance.

On the basis of a very close study of this type of situation in an American gypsum mine, Gouldner has described the effects of the introduction of bureaucratic organization in the face of opposition. The previous management system of the mine was based on 'the indulgency pattern'. The rules were ignored or applied very leniently; the men were infrequently checked on and were always given a second chance if infringements came to light. There was a very relaxed atmosphere and a favourable attitude of the workers to the company. Into this situation came the new mine manager who set about seeing that the rules were enforced, that the authority structure functioned effectively, and in general that an efficient rational–legal organization was operated. But this also resulted in a great drop in morale and increased management–worker conflict – including a wildcat strike.

In his analysis of this situation Gouldner was able to distinguish three patterns of bureaucratic behaviour: mock, representative and punishment-centred – each with its characteristic values and conflicts.

In *mock bureaucracy* the rules are imposed on the group by some outside agency: for example, a rule laid down by an insurance company forbidding smoking in a shop, or official returns required outside the organization on the activities of members. Neither superiors nor subordinates identify themselves with or participate in the establishment of the rules, nor do they regard them as legitimate. Thus the rules are not enforced, and both superiors and subordinates obtain status by violating them. Smoking is allowed unless an outside inspector is present; purely formal returns are made, giving no indication of the real state of affairs. The actual position differs very much from the official position and people may spend a lot of time 'going through the motions'. This behaviour pattern of mock bureaucracy corresponds with the common conception of bureaucratic 'red tape' administration which is divorced from reality. However, in such a system, as Gouldner points out, morale may be very high since the informal values and attitudes of all participants are bolstered by the joint violation or evasion of the rules in order to get on with 'the real job'.

In *representative bureaucracy* Gouldner takes up and develops one strand of Weber's concept, the situation in which rules are promulgated by 'experts' whose authority is acceptable to all the members of the organization. Superiors and subordinates support the rules which fit in with their values and confer status on those who conform. For example, pressure may come from both management and workers to develop a safety programme; a high quality of workmanship may be expected and achieved. In this situation rules are enforced by superiors and obeyed by subordinates, perhaps with some tension but with little overt conflict. As the values are held in common by all, deviations are explained by well-intentioned carelessness or ignorance, since it would not be thought possible that the values are disputed. The joint support for the rules is buttressed by feelings of solidarity and participation in a joint enterprise. This behaviour pattern of representative bureaucracy corresponds very closely to the ideal forms of organization strongly advocated by such writers as Taylor and Fayol (see pp. 133–7 and pp. 63–7) in which authority is based not on position but on accepted knowledge and expertise.

In the third type of bureaucracy, *punishment-centred*, the rules arise in response to the pressures of *either* management *or* workers. The attempt is made to coerce the other side into compliance. For example, management may introduce stricter control on production, clocking-in procedures and fines. This type of bureaucracy emphasizes the elements of authority and command – hierarchy in Weber's concept – although, as Gouldner points out, there can be a power struggle in which the solidarity of the subordinates imposes rules on the management, e.g. job demarcation rules, overtime bans, rigid redundancy procedures. Either superiors or subordinates consider the rules legitimate, and if conformity leads to a gain in status for one side this involves a loss in status for the other. Deviation from the rules is not explained away as in representative bureaucracy, but is regarded as wilful disobedience. Such a situation clearly entails much conflict and tension.

The patterns of behaviour characteristic of these three 'types of bureaucracy' may coexist in different degrees in any one organization, and they are perhaps better described as 'modes of bureaucratic functioning'. The punishment-centred mode, which is the most frequently used, is intended to produce an efficient organization working in conformity to rationally designed rules and procedures. It emphasizes the use of general and impersonal rules, which decrease the emphasis on the personal power of those in authority. This in turn leads to a reduction in interpersonal tension which promotes efficiency and reinforces the use of impersonal bureaucratic rules. This is the strength of bureaucracy – as Weber pointed out.

But Gouldner maintains that there are unanticipated consequences of bureaucratic functioning which Weber left out of account. General and impersonal rules, by their very nature, define what is *not* allowed and thus increase people's knowledge of what is the minimum acceptable behaviour, which tends to become the standard behaviour. This lowers efficiency and, in a punishment-centred bureaucracy, leads to increased closeness of supervision to see that the rules are carried out, and as a consequence to increased emphasis on authority and greater interpersonal tension. This results in the continued issue of formal impersonal rules to deal with the conflicts, and the cycle then begins again. Thus both the anticipated and unanticipated consequences of bureaucracy lead to a reinforcement of bureaucratic behaviour. The system is essentially unstable, achieving its goals only at the cost of much interpersonal tension and conflict.

Thus, rules have both positive and negative effects, anticipated and unanticipated consequences. An overall aim of rules is to overcome the effect of close supervision which makes power differences too visible and thereby may offend norms of equality. So rules serve as an equivalent for direct orders by providing a statement of the obligations of a particular job (their explicational function). However, in certain circumstances the informal group may provide this function, thereby leading to unanticipated consequences of conflict. Rules also provide an impersonal way of using authority (their screening function). Along with this, rules enable control to take place at a distance (their remote control function). But here again, the distance may get too great, leading to a 'mock' situation of authority. Rules also constitute a definition of expectation, together with sanctions for non-performance (their punishment-legitimating function). But rules also define minimal standards allowing individuals to work at low levels of commitment (their apathy-preserving function). It is the different possibilities in the operation of rules which provide the dysfunctions of bureaucracy.

Gouldner has also been concerned to distinguish different outlooks among administrators and to show the effects these have upon their attitudes to their jobs, their employing organizations, their professions and their colleagues. This arises from a further criticism of Weber. Gouldner suggests that there is an inherent contradiction in bureaucracy between a system of authority based on the appointment of experts, and authority based on hierarchy and discipline. In the first case authority is legitimized because of superior knowledge; in the second it arises from the office held. This represents a particular incompatibility in those organizations which employ large numbers of professionals who may have more technical knowledge than their hierarchical superiors. Gouldner distinguishes two main categories of administrators: *cosmopolitans* and *locals*. Cosmopolitans are administrators with little loyalty to the organization, but much committed to their specialized skills. They have an extremely professional outlook. They think of themselves primarily as engineers or accountants, for instance. Locals are administrators with great loyalty to the organization, but with little commitment to specialized skills. They think of themselves as 'company men'. Although organizations wish to retain the loyalty of their personnel (and therefore, for example, to promote by seniority from within) they also have a basic rational orientation towards efficiency (which requires appointment by skill and competence from wherever it is obtainable). This built-in dilemma is another major cause of tension in the modern organization.

Gouldner has contrasted mechanical systems with natural systems such as societies, institutions and organizations. People within natural systems are not just empty shells constrained by the circumstances in which they find themselves; they have ideas, perceptions and choices to make as they operate the system, which shape the organization structure, often away from the intentions of the designers. For Gouldner social science has the special role in society of offering an explanatory and critical approach to organizations and institutions in order to help in this process and thus proclaim the autonomy of man.

Bibliography

Gouldner, A. W., *Patterns of Industrial Bureaucracy,* New York: Free Press, 1954.

Gouldner, A. W., *Wildcat Strike,* New York: Free Press, 1954.

Gouldner, A. W., 'Cosmopolitans and locals: towards an analysis of latent social roles, I', *Administrative Science Quarterly* I (1957), 281-306.

Gouldner, A. W., 'Organizational Analysis', in R. K. Merton *et al.* (eds.), *Sociology Today,* New York: Basic Books, 1958.

Joan Woodward

Joan Woodward (1916–1971) was Professor of Industrial Sociology at the Imperial College of Science and Technology, University of London. She began her research career at the University of Liverpool, but she is best known for her subsequent work on technology and organization in manufacturing firms as director of the Human Relations Research Unit at the South-East Essex Technical College. She and her colleagues at Imperial College broadened and deepened this line of research.

From 1953 to 1957 Woodward led the South-East Essex research team in a survey of manufacturing organizations in that area (see Woodward, 1958, 1965). In all, a hundred firms participated; though the amount of information obtained on them varied from firm to firm, and the published information is therefore on smaller numbers. Firms ranged in size from a hundred employees to over a thousand, and some were the main establishments of their companies whilst others were branch factories. The survey was supplemented by intensive studies of selected firms.

Woodward does not use sweeping classifications of organizations by types (such as those suggested by Weber – charismatic, traditionalistic, bureaucratic – or by Burns – organismic, mechanistic). Rather than attempt in this way to summate whole ranges of characteristics of organizations, she investigates specific features such as the number of levels of authority between top and bottom, the span of control or average number of subordinates of supervisors, the clarity or otherwise with which duties are defined, the amount of written communication, and the extent of division of functions among specialists

Woodward finds that firms show considerable differences in features such as these. Foremen may have to supervise anything from a handful to eighty or ninety workers; the number of levels of management in production departments may be anywhere from two to eight; communication can be almost entirely verbal or largely written. Why should these differences occur?

Woodward's team compared firms of different sizes, and examined differences in historical background, without finding any answer. But when differences in technology were studied, relationships were seen with many organizational features. It is not claimed as a result that technology is the only influence upon a firm's organization nor that individual managers make no impression, but technology is a major factor.

Woodward finds that the objectives of a firm – what it wishes to make, and for what markets – determine the kind of technology it uses. For example, a firm building novel prototypes of electronic equipment could not do so by the techniques of mass production which dominate vehicle manufacture. Production systems differ in their degree of technical complexity, from unit (jobbing) and small batch production, through large batch and mass production to the most complex, namely process production.

These three broad categories are sub-divided into nine sub-categories of production systems (see Woodward, 1958 for an earlier slightly different version) from least to most complex:

Unit and small batch
1. Production of units to customers' requirements.
2. Production of prototypes.
3. Fabrication of large equipments in stages.
4. Production of small batches to customers' orders.

Large batch and mass production
5. Production of large batches.
6. Production of large batches on assembly lines.
7. Mass production.

Process production
8. Intermittent production of chemicals in multi-purpose plant.
9. Continuous flow production of liquids, gases and crystalline substances.

Some firms used more than one of these production systems and so were placed in additional 'combined system' categories. A distinguishing feature of process systems is that they manufacture products measured by dimensions of weight or volume (e.g. liquids) rather than those usually counted as series of integral units (e.g. numbers of vehicles or of packaged goods).

In general, the higher the category the more it is possible to exercise control over the manufacturing operations because performance can be pre-determined. In a continuous-flow plant such as a chemical installation the equipment can be set for a given result; capacity and breakdown probabilities are known. But in batch production full capacity may not be known and even well-developed production control procedures represent a continual attempt to set fresh targets in the face of many uncertainties of day-to-day manufacture. In unit production of prototypes, for example, it is almost impossible to predict the results of development work.

These differences in technology account for many differences in organization structure. In process technologies where equipment does the job, taller hierarchies are found with longer lines of command, but managed through committees rather than by instruction down the line. Such hierarchies include more trained university graduates; and since the proportion of personnel working directly on production is low, the hierarchy of administrative and managerial personnel is a comparatively large proportion of total employees.

Despite the complex administrative hierarchy of specialist staff and control departments common in large batch and mass production technologies, these have shorter lines of command and proportionately fewer managers and clerks. Their salient characteristic is large numbers of direct production operatives.

Unit and small batch production typically has an even shorter hierarchy where no manager is very far from the production work itself. This relies relatively heavily upon the production personnel themselves without extensive administrative controls.

Some organization characteristics do not differ straight along the nine technology categories. On some, large batch and mass production is often distinctive whilst unit and process production have much in common with each other. The large numbers of semi-skilled workers on which mass production is based mean that the span of control of supervisors is very wide, and since results are obtained through the pressure exerted by bosses upon subordinates, human and industrial relations may be strained. Typical of both unit and process production are comparatively small groups of skilled workers with more personal relationships with their supervisors.

Similarly, the complex production control problems of large batch and mass systems are reflected in their numbers of staff specialists, greater paperwork, and attempted clear-cut definition of duties, leading to more mechanistic organizations as Burns (p. 32) has called them.

A rough assessment of the firms on both financial and market performance and on reputation showed that the apparently more successful firms had organizational characteristics near the median or average for their category of technology. Perhaps there is one form of organization most appropriate to each system of production. Successful process firms must have taller, more narrowly based, organization pyramids; successful unit production firms must have relatively short pyramids; and so on.

Certainly more prolonged case-studies carried out by Woodward and her colleagues to test out the results of the initial survey showed that a change of technology category seems to force changes in organization. This in itself may bring conflict among those whose interests are affected, especially if the change is into batch type production. Firms were studied which moved from unit to batch, attempts being made to rationalize and increase the scale of production; and from process to batch, where for example a firm began to package a product previously sold in bulk. In such cases, middle managers and supervisors find that in batch production their days disappear in a confusion of calls and contacts with other people, that this subjects them to greater personal stress, and that their responsibility for production overlaps with that of new planning and control departments.

Indeed, such changes in technology may alter the whole status of the several functions in a firm. This is because the cycle of manufacture places development, production and marketing in a different order in different technologies. In unit or jobbing systems, marketing precedes development and production follows last, since not until a customer requires a product and it is designed can production occur. In large batch and mass systems, the development and production of a new line precedes its mass marketing. In process systems, development of a possible product and marketing to assured customers must precede commitment of capital to special purpose plant to produce it. In each system, the most critical function is the central one which has the greatest effect on success. That is, in unit systems, development has most importance and status; in mass systems it is production; in process systems it is marketing.

Woodward and her colleagues have carried out further detailed case studies of managerial control in its various forms as the link between the technology of manufacture and organizational structure and behaviour. In *Industrial Organization: Behaviour and Control*, Reeves and Woodward focus upon two dimensions of managerial control systems: first, the extent to which control varies between being personal and impersonal; secondly, the degree to which control is fragmented.

Along the first dimension, there is a range of control systems from completely personal hierarchical control at one extreme, as operated by an owner-employer, to completely impersonal mechanical control at the other, as operated by measurement mechanisms and the automatic controls of machine tools. In the middle of the range come the impersonal control processes which are based on administrative procedures, such as production planning and cost systems. Firms may be compared along this dimension, which is associated with characteristic effects upon structure and behaviour. The most important effect is that movement towards impersonal control involves a separation between the planning and execution stages of the work process.

At the personal end of the scale there is almost total overlap between planning and execution; with impersonal administrative control processes there is considerable separation but the planning departments such as production control, quality control and cost control are involved in the execution of the work; at the mechanical end of the scale there can be total separation – the control designers and planners not being concerned at all with the operations since they have already built in correction mechanisms at the planning stage. Indeed the planning and design stages at the mechanical control end of the scale may be the concern of a separate organization, as when a chemical engineering firm undertakes the design and erection of an automated continuous-flow chemical plant complete with mechanical control processes, which is then handed over to the contracting organization.

The second dimension of control systems studied by Reeves and Woodward was the extent to which control was fragmented, ranging from a single integrated system of control at one extreme, to multi-system fragmented control at the other. To obtain a single integrated system, a firm would continuously attempt to relate the standards set for various departments to the performance and adjustment mechanisms associated with them. At the other end of the scale, a firm might have a number of control criteria operating independently which are continuously reconciled by the supervisor or the production operative. A job has to be done by a particular date as set by production control, to a particular standard as set by quality control, to a cost limit as set by cost control, by particular methods as set by work study, and so on. An inevitable result of having a multiplicity of systems with fragmented control is conflict, when the supervisor attempts to satisfy each of the control criteria and in doing so jeopardizes his performance on the others.

The two dimensions of control processes are used together to generate a four-fold typology of systems in a developmental sequence. Four categories are outlined:

1. Firms with unitary and mainly personal controls, such as an entrepreneurial firm, where the owner would himself relate time and quality to cost. This type is characteristic of unit and small batch production.
2. Firms with fragmented and mainly personal controls, such as a firm where more individuals were involved in setting control criteria.
3. Firms with fragmented and mainly impersonal administrative or mechanical controls, such as a firm where the control criteria are impersonally set by functional departments. Most large batch and mass production firms fall here or in category 2.
4. Firms with unitary and mainly impersonal administrative or mechanical controls, such as a firm controlling the total manufacturing process to a master plan, perhaps using a computer for information processing and process control. This type is characteristic of process production.

The basic assumption and conclusion of Woodward's work is that meaningful explanations of differences in organization and behaviour can be found in the work situation itself. The technology of this work situation should be a critical consideration in management practice. There is no one best way. She warns against accepting principles of administration as universally applicable. The same principles can produce different results in different circumstances; many principles derive from experience of large batch or mass production only and are not likely to apply in other technologies. Careful study of the objectives and technology of a firm is required.

Woodward's study pioneered both in empirical investigation and in setting a fresh framework of thought. Prior to it, thinking about organization depended on the apt but often over-generalized statements of experienced managers, and on isolated case-studies of particular firms. Woodward showed the possibilities of comparisons of large numbers of firms so that generalizations might be securely based and their limits seen.

She forces thinking away from the abstract elaboration of principles of administration to an examination of the constraints placed on organization structure and management practice by differing technologies and their associated control systems.

Bibliography

Woodward, J., *The Dock Worker,* Liverpool University Press, 1955.

Woodward, J., 'Management and technology', *Problems of Progress in Industry* 3, HMSO, 1958.

Woodward, J., *The Saleswoman: A Study of Attitudes and Behaviour in Retail Distribution,* Pitman, 1960.

Woodward, J., *Industrial Organization: Theory and Practice,* Oxford University Press, 1965, 2nd edn 1980.

Woodward, J. (ed.), *Industrial Organization: Behaviour and Control,* Oxford University Press, 1970.

Tom Burns

Tom Burns spent more than thirty years at the university of Edinburgh, retiring in 1981 as Professor of Sociology. His early interests were in urban sociology and he worked with the West Midland Group on Post-war Reconstruction and Planning. While he was at Edinburgh his particular concern was with studies of different types of organization and their effects on communication patterns and on the activities of managers. He has also explored the relevance of different forms of organization to changing conditions – especially to the impact of technical innovation.

In collaboration with a psychologist (G. M. Stalker), Burns has studied the attempt to introduce electronics development work into traditional Scottish firms, with a view to their entering this modern and rapidly expanding industry as the markets for their own well-established products diminished. The difficulties which these firms faced in adjusting to the new situation of continuously changing technology and markets led him to describe two 'ideal types' of management organization which are the extreme points of a continuum along which most organizations can be placed.

The *mechanistic* type of organization is adapted to relatively stable conditions. In it the problems and tasks of management are broken down into specialisms within which each individual carries out his assigned, precisely defined, task. There is a clear hierarchy of control, and the responsibility for overall knowledge and co-ordination rests exclusively at the top of the hierarchy. Vertical communication and interaction (i.e. between superiors and subordinates) is emphasized, and there is an insistence on loyalty to the concern and obedience to superiors. This system corresponds quite closely to Weber's rational–legal bureaucracy (see p. 17).

The *organismic* (also called *organic*) type of organization is adapted to unstable conditions when new and unfamiliar problems continually arise which cannot be broken down and distributed among the existing specialist roles. There is therefore a continual adjustment and redefinition of individual tasks and the contributive rather than restrictive nature of specialist knowledge is emphasized. Interactions and communication (information and advice rather than orders) may occur at any level as required by the process, and a much higher degree of commitment to the aims of the organization as a whole is generated. In this system, organization charts laying down the exact functions and responsibilities of each individual are not found, and indeed their use may be explicitly rejected as hampering the efficient functioning of the organization.

The almost complete failure of the traditional Scottish firms to absorb electronics research and development engineers into their organizations leads Burns to doubt whether a mechanistic firm can consciously change to an organismic one. This is because the individual in a mechanistic organization is not only committed to the organization as a whole. He is also a member of a group or department with a stable career structure and with sectional interests in conflict with those of other groups. Thus there develop power struggles between established sections to obtain control of the new functions and resources. These divert the organization from purposive adaptation and allow out-of-date mechanistic structures to be perpetuated and 'pathological' systems to develop.

Pathological systems are attempts by mechanistic organizations to cope with new problems of change, innovation and uncertainty while sticking to the formal bureaucratic structure. Burns describes three of these typical reactions. In a mechanistic organization the normal procedure for dealing with a matter outside an individual's sphere of responsibility is to refer it to the appropriate specialist or, failing that, to a superior. In a rapidly changing situation the need for such consultations occurs frequently; and in many instances the superior has to put up the matter higher still. A heavy load of such decisions finds its way to the chief executive, and it soon becomes apparent that many decisions can only be made by going to the top. Thus there develops the *ambiguous figure system* of an official hierarchy and a non-officially-recognized system of pair relationships between the chief executive and some dozens of people at different positions below him in the management structure. The head of the concern is overloaded with work, and many senior managers whose status depends on the functioning of the formal system feel frustrated at being by-passed.

Some firms attempted to cope with the problems of communication by creating more branches of the bureaucratic hierarchy, e.g. contract managers, liaison officers. This leads to a system described as the *mechanistic jungle*, in which a new job or even a whole new department may be created, whose existence depends on the perpetuation of these difficulties. The third type of pathological response is the *super-personal* or *committee system*. The committee is the traditional way of dealing with temporary problems which cannot be solved within a single individual's role, without upsetting the balance of power. But as a permanent device it is inefficient, in that it has to compete with the loyalty demanded and career structure offered by the traditional departments. This system was tried only sporadically by the firms, since it was disliked as being typical of inefficient government administration; attempts to develop the committee as a super-person to fulfil a continuing function that no individual could carry out met with little success.

For a proper understanding of organizational functioning, Burns maintains, it is therefore always necessary to conceive of organizations as the simultaneous working of at least three social systems. The first of these is the formal authority system derived from the aims of the organization, its technology, its attempts to cope with its environment. This is the overt system in terms of which all discussion about decision-making takes place. But organizations are also cooperative systems of people who have career aspirations and a career structure, and who compete for advancement. Thus decisions taken in the overt structure inevitably affect the differential career prospects of the members, who will therefore evaluate them in terms of the career system as well as the formal system, and will react accordingly. This leads to the third system of relationships which is part of an organization – its political system. Every organization is the scene of 'political' activity in which individuals and departments compete and cooperate for power. Again all decisions in the overt system are evaluated for their relative impact on the power structure as well as for their contribution to the achievement of the organization's goals.

It is naive to consider the organization as a unitary system equated with the formal system, and any change to be successful must be acceptable in terms of the career structure and the political structure as well. This is particularly so with modern technologically based organizations which contain qualified experts who have a career structure and a technical authority which goes far beyond the organization itself and its top management. Thus the attempt to change from a mechanistic to an organismic management structure has enormous implications for the career structure (which is much less dependent on the particular organization) and the power system (which is much more diffuse deriving from technical knowledge as much as formal position).

Concern with the interaction of these three social systems within the organization continues in Burns's study of the BBC. The BBC is a very segmented organization both horizontally, where there are a large number of departments (e.g. Drama, Outside Broadcasts, Finance) who appear to be competing as much as cooperating, and vertically, where in order to rise in the grading structure the executive soon loses contact with the professional skills (e.g. journalism, engineering) which he is supposed to administer. In this situation the career and the political systems can become more important than the formal task system.

Burns charts the rise in power of the central management of the BBC at the expense of the creative and professional staff, which stems from the Corporation's financial pressures. He maintains that the Corporation can only develop as a creative service dedicated to the public good, if it is freed from its financial client relationship to the government.

'A sense of the past and the very recent past is essential to anyone who is trying to perceive the here-and-now of industrial organization.' If the organizational structure is viewed as a result of a process of continuous development of the three social systems of formal organization, career structure and political system, a study of this process will help organizations to avoid traps they would otherwise fall into. Adaptation to new and changing situations is not automatic. Indeed many factors militate against it. An important one is the existence of an organization structure appropriate to an earlier phase of development. Another is the multi-faceted nature of an organization member's commitment to his career, his department, his sub-unit, as well as to the organization as a whole.

Bibliography

Burns, T., 'Industry in a new age.' *New Society,* 31 January 1963, no. 18. Reprinted in D. S. Pugh (ed.), *Organization Theory,* 2nd edn, New York: Viking-Penguin, 1984.

Burns, T., 'On the plurality of social systems', in J. R. Lawrence (ed.), *Operational Research and the Social Sciences,* Tavistock, 1966.

Burns, T., *The BBC: Public Institution and Private World,* Macmillan, 1977.

Burns, T., and Stalker, G. M., *The Management of Innovation,* London: Tavistock, 1966, 2nd edn 1968.

Derek Pugh and the Aston Group

In the late 1950s, Derek Pugh, now Professor of Systems at the Open University, England, brought to the Birmingham College of Advanced Technology (which became the University of Aston-in-Birmingham) a distinctive view of how to conduct research. His research experience as a social psychologist at the University of Edinburgh had placed him in close contact with researchers in other social sciences. He believed that the scope of empirical investigation and of understanding could be widened by multidisciplinary research, founded on a common commitment to and ownership of results within the research team, and on team management skills.

The Industrial Administration Research Unit at Aston led by Pugh between 1961 and 1970 included several 'generations' of researchers whose academic origins ranged from psychology, sociology, economics and politics, to no specific discipline at all. The names which appear most frequently on publications are John Child, David Hickson, Bob Hinings, Roy Payne, Diana Pheysey, and Charles McMillan as the initiator with David Hickson of much subsequent international research, but there are many more. It is symptomatic of the nature of the group that it has not taken on the name of any one individual, even that of Derek Pugh, but is usually known as the Aston Group, even though there is no longer any special link with that University. The programme of research dispersed with the members of the group, and they and others in touch with them have pursued its work elsewhere in Britain and in several other countries.

The Aston Programme contributed to organization theory by blending some of the research methods and assumptions of psychology with conceptions of organizations and their workings from sociology and economics. Its approach has three essential elements. First, because organizations and their members are changing and complex, numbers of their *attributes should be studied together and as matters of degree*, not as 'either/or' phenomena – a multi-variate approach to a changing world of greys, rather than blacks and whites. This also implies that there will be no single reason for the way in which an organization is set up and run, but many possible influences (i.e. multi-variate causal explanation). What happens cannot be due to an organization's size alone, nor for that matter to its technology alone, but must in some degree be due to a number of these and other factors all acting together.

Second, because organizations outlast the comings and goings of individuals, it is *appropriate to study their non-personal or institutional aspects* using information on their divisions of work, their control systems and their formal hierarchies. For this, individuals can be interviewed as informants who describe these aspects, rather than being asked to indicate how they experience the organization personally, which they would be if asked to respond to questionnaires about themselves.

Third, because organizations are working wholes, they and their members *should be seen from more than one perspective* to give the fullest possible view. 'The response to the recurring conundrum "does man make organization or does organization make man?" must be to assume that both are happening all the time.' Therefore, the Aston Programme aimed to link:

1. Organizational structure and functioning
2. Group composition and interaction
3. Individual personality and behaviour

Early ambitions to include features of the surrounding society were not realized initially, but began to be included later, when research extended beyond Britain to organizations in other societies.

The Programme commenced with a project in the Birmingham area in England, from which has grown all further research. It focused on the organizational level by studying a highly diverse sample of forty-six organizations: private sector and public sector, from manufacturers of cars and chocolate bars to municipal departments, public services and chain stores. Their formal structures were analysed in terms of their degrees of:

Specialization of functions and roles;
Standardization of procedures;
Formalization of documentation;
Centralization of authority;
Configuration of role structure.

These concepts reflect prevalent ideas about bureaucratization and how to manage, which can be found in the work of Weber (p. 15) and Fayol (p. 63).

A very large number of ways of measuring these aspects of structure were devised which have been employed variously by many researchers since. The most distinctive kind of measure used, an innovation in research on organizations, was based on demonstrating that, for example, the number of functions (such as finance or public relations) that an organization had specialized out of possible specialisms could validly be added to give it a specialization score, and similarly with standardization, formalization, and centralization. This enabled one organization to be compared with another in these terms for the first time.

Despite the range and ramifications of this research, its salient results took on a relatively simple outline. First, each measure of specialization, standardization and formalization was simplified into a combined score for each organization. To distinguish this from its three constituents, it was called *structuring of activities*. An organization with highly structured activities has many specialized sections such as buying, training, work study and so on, and many routine procedures and formal documents, the total effect being that what has to be done is marked out or structured. Second, centralization of decision making and the autonomy of an organization's decision making from any owning organization were together termed *concentration of authority*. An organization with concentrated authority not only has most of its decisions taken at the top of its own hierarchy but has many decisions taken for it, over its head, by the management of another organization of which it is a wholly or partly owned subsidiary or subordinate section.

Thus at its simplest, the Aston Group isolated two primary elements of any organization, how far the activities of its personnel are structured and how far its decision-making authority is concentrated at the top, which between them sum up much of what an organization is like. Know them and you know it, to a large extent, for they are its two fundamentals.

Although the Aston Programme's approach assumes that organizations are what they are for many reasons, these first results were also relatively simple in the principal explanations that they suggested. A series of features including an organization's purpose, ownership, technology, size and dependence were examined for any correlation with how far an organization had structured its activities or concentrated its authority. It was found that ownership (whether private or public, dispersed in thousands of shareholdings or in the hands of a family) made little difference to structuring and concentration; as did technology, which was reflected in only a few aspects of structure (this qualified and limited the import of Woodward's work (p. 25).

What did and does matter much more for the form taken by an organization is its *size*, and its degree of *dependence upon other organizations*. The larger it is the more likely its employees are to work in very specialized functions, following standardized procedures and formalized documentation; that is, it will score highly on structuring of activities and have many of the appearances of bureaucracy. The more it is dependent upon only a few owning, supplier, or customer units, or even just one – total dependence is where an organization is wholly owned by another which supplies all its needs and takes all its outputs – the less autonomy it will have in its own decision making, and even those decisions that are left to it are likely to be centralized within itself rather than decentralized.

Yet these results, substantially supported in many later projects, did not mean a working world immovably fixed by a few major elements. Not only did all of these elements change all the time – for organizations grow in size and abolish some formalized documents and introduce others – but all these and the other elements studied were open to *strategic choice*. Indeed, they had all in some sense been chosen, and were continually being chosen. Managers and administrators choose whether or not an organization is to grow or to enter into contracts that make it dependent upon others. They choose the means of management and control which structure its activities and concentrate its authority. But *one choice constrains another* – each choice (e.g. of size) constrains the options open for the next (e.g. of the degree of structuring to be adopted). A major instance of this is that the choice of how far to develop either of the two primary elements, structuring and concentration, is likely to limit to some extent what can be done with the other, for there is a small negative relationship between them; that is, more of one probably means somewhat less of the other, and to that extent they are alternative means of controlling an organization – not mutually exclusive alternatives (since all organizations use both) but alternative emphases.

Since the first Birmingham area project, the Aston Programme's research in Britain has moved from the original sample of numerous kinds of organization to samples of one kind only such as business firms, trade unions, local governments, and churches, to investigate their particular characteristics. It has extended to other European nations, to the United States and Canada, to Japan, and to the Middle East and India. Broadly, the results have shown the same overall pattern between similar major factors, but differences have been found that characterize local government and educational institutions, for instance, and also particular nations (organizations in Poland are remarkably centralized, for example, while high structuring in Japan reflects modern management methods).

Casting their results into an empirically derived taxonomy of forms of organization structure, the Aston Group put forward from their first project a view of the forms prevalent in contemporary industrialized society, in Britain and probably elsewhere too. Large firms, big businesses are typically *workflow bureaucracies*, highly structured but not as highly concentrated in authority as some. Public service organizations of local and central government are *personnel bureaucracies*, not very structured but with highly concentrated authority and procedures focused on hiring, promoting and firing of personnel. Smaller units within large private or public groups are *full bureaucracies*, with the high structuring of the workflow type and the highly concentrated authority of the personnel type. Smaller firms in personal ownership have neither of these features to any great extent, being *non-bureaucracies* (or implicitly structured). There are other types, but these four main ones can be depicted thus:

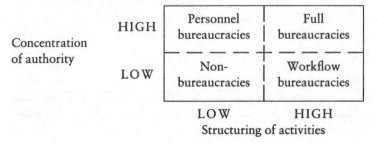

		Structuring of activities	
		LOW	HIGH
Concentration of authority	HIGH	Personnel bureaucracies	Full bureaucracies
	LOW	Non-bureaucracies	Workflow bureaucracies

The progression of the Aston Group into research on group and role characteristics and on the individual's experience of organizational 'climate', in accordance with their Programme of linking organizational, group, and individual levels of analysis, is not so well known. Its results are not so clear cut. If any construction can be placed on them overall, it is that they lift from bureaucracy the pall of gloom laid over it by widespread assumptions of its uniformly stifling and dreary nature. It may be like that: but if it is, then it is for those in the lowest-level jobs and not necessarily for those higher in the hierarchy. Life for them differs from one bureaucratic organization to another.

Through a mixture of surveys and of intensive case studies with batteries of methods, Aston researchers showed that whilst structuring of activities does tend to be associated with greater formality at the group interaction level, and concentration of authority does tend to be associated with less autonomy for individuals and with greater conventional attention to rules, nevertheless a uniformly bureaucratic-type firm can be effective and its personnel can like working in it. At least, this was so in their case study of a small firm owned by a large international corporation, a 'small effective bureaucracy' which they code-named 'Aston'.

In organizations that showed both high structuring and high concentration of authority, which were loosely equated with bureaucracies, there was no evidence of less attractive 'climates' (in terms of the way in which authority was exercised, of interest in work, of routine, and of personal relationships). At the top, such organizations tended to have managers who were younger and better qualified, with more flexible and challenging attitudes. And firms with younger managers tended to show faster growth in sales and assets (though whether youth caused growth or growth attracted younger personnel is an unanswered question). So those managing more bureaucratic-type firms were unlikely themselves to be cautious and conformist, and were more likely to seek innovation and risk.

Greater confidence is shown in the Aston Programme's achievements at the organization level of analysis, however. While it must be remembered that much of their data is on whether procedures, documents and defined authority are there or are not there, whether the means of control are ready for use, and do not tell how far these means are then used, the Programme demonstrated that significant comparisons between organizations of virtually any kind could be made in these terms. It provided usable concepts and measures of organization structure that have withstood use and re-use.

Bibliography

Pugh, D. S., and Hickson, D. J., *Organizational Structure in its Context: The Aston Programme I,* Brookfield, VT: Gower Publishing, 1976.

Pugh, D. S., and Hinings, C. R. (eds.), *Organizational Structure—Extensions and Replications: The Aston Programme II,* Brookfield, VT: Gower Publishing, 1976.

Pugh, D. S., and Payne, R. L. (eds.), *Organizational Behaviour in its Context: The Aston Programme III,* Brookfield, VT: Gower Publishing, 1977.

Hickson, D. J., and McMillan, C. J. (eds.), *Organization and Nation: The Aston Programme IV,* Brookfield, VT: Gower Publishing, 1981.

Paul Lawrence and Jay Lorsch

Paul Lawrence and Jay Lorsch are professorial colleagues in Organizational Behaviour at the Harvard Business School, where Lawrence has taught for well over thirty years and Lorsch since 1965. Together with many collaborators (who include S. A. Allan, S. M. Davis, J. Kotter, H. Lane, and J. J. Morse) they have for nearly two decades been conducting a series of studies into the appropriate structure and functioning of organizations using what has become known as the 'organization and environment' approach, described in their seminal book of that title.

Lawrence and Lorsch begin their analysis with the question of why men seek to build organizations. Their answer, which follows and builds on the work of Barnard (p. 68) is that organizations enable people to find better solutions to the environmental problems facing them. This immediately highlights three key elements in their approach to understanding organizational behaviour: (1) it is people who have purposes, not organizations; (2) people have to come together to coordinate their different activities into an organization; and (3) the effectiveness of the organization is judged by the adequacy with which the members' needs are satisfied through planned transactions with the environment.

It is in order to cope effectively with their external environments that organizations must come to develop segmented units, each of which has as its major task the problem of dealing with some aspect of the conditions outside the firm. For example, in a manufacturing firm with production, sales and design units, the production unit deals with production equipment sources, raw materials sources and labour markets; the sales unit faces problems with the market, the customers and the competitors; the design unit has to cope with technological developments, government regulations and so on. This *differentiation* of function and task is accompanied by differences in cognitive and emotional orientation among the managers in different units, and differences, too, in the formal structure of different departments. For instance the development department may have a long-term time horizon and a very informal structure, whereas production may be dealing with day-to-day problems in a rigidly formal system, with sales facing the medium-term effects of competitors' advertising with moderate formality.

In spite of this the organization is a system which has to be coordinated so that a state of collaboration exists in order to obtain for members the benefits of effective transactions with the environment. This is the required *integration* and it, too, is affected by the nature of the external conditions.

The basic necessity for *both* appropriate differentiation *and* adequate integration to perform effectively in the external environment is at the core of Lawrence and Lorsch's model of organizational functioning. The approach was developed in an important study which they carried out on ten firms in three different industries – plastics (six firms), food (two firms) and containers (two firms) – which constituted very different environments for the enterprises concerned.

The study recognized that all the firms involved segment their environment. Each of the ten was dealing with a market sub-environment (the task of the sales department), a techno-economic sub-environment (the task of the manufacturing unit) and a scientific sub-environment (the task of the R&D, or design department). The greater the degree of uncertainty within each sub-environment and the greater the diversity between them, the greater was the need of the firms to *differentiate* between their sub-units of sales, production and research in order to be effective in each sub-environment. For example in the plastics industry, which was found to have great diversity, with the science sub-environment highly uncertain but the techno-economic one relatively stable, a considerable degree of differentiation within effective firms was found. In the container industry, on the other hand, all parts of the environment were relatively certain and so a much lower degree of differentiation was apparent.

But greater differentiation brings with it potential for greater inter-departmental conflict as the specialist groups develop their own ways of dealing with the particular uncertainties of their own sub-environments. These differences are not just minor variations in outlook but may involve fundamental ways of thinking and behaving. In the plastics industry a sales manager may be discussing a potential new product in terms of whether it will perform in his customers' machinery, whether they will pay the cost and whether he can get it on the market in three months' time. The research scientist at the same meeting may be thinking about whether he could change the molecular structure of the material without affecting its stability and whether doing this would open out a line of research for the next two years which would be more interesting than another project he heard about yesterday. These two specialists not only think differently, they dress differently, they have different habits of punctuality and so on. It therefore becomes crucial that a highly differentiated firm should have appropriate methods of *integration* and conflict resolution if they are to perform well in the environment.

The table below lists the integrative devices which were found to be operating in three high-performing organizations, one from each of the industries studied. The top row gives the rating for the degree of differentiation, and it will be seen that the need to operate effectively in the plastics environment led the firm to develop a high degree of differentiation; the container firm had the lowest differentiation and the food firm was in between.

Comparison of Integrative Devices in Three High-performing Organizations

	Plastics	*Food*	*Container*
Degree of differentiation	10.7	8.0	5.7
Major integrative devices	(1) Integrative department	(1) Individual integrators	(1) Direct managerial contact
	(2) Permanent cross-functional teams at three levels of management	(2) Temporary cross-functional teams	(2) Managerial hierarchy
	(3) Direct managerial contact	(3) Direct managerial contact	(3) Paper system
	(4) Managerial hierarchy	(4) Managerial hierarchy	
	(5) Paper system	(5) Paper system	

from Lawrence and Lorsch (1967)

Each of these firms used a different combination of devices for achieving integration. All of them used to some extent the traditional methods of paper systems, the formal managerial hierarchy and direct managerial contact between members of the different departments. For the container firm with the least differentiation these methods were sufficient but in the food firm, which had a greater need for integration, temporary teams made up of specialists from the units involved were set up to deal with a particularly urgent issue. Managers within functional departments were also assigned integrating roles such as that of liaison officer. Clearly the effective food firm was devoting a larger amount of time and effort to integrating activity.

The plastics organization had in addition established a special department one of whose primary activities was integration. They also had an elaborate set of permanent integrating teams, each made up of members from the various functional units and the integrating department. The purpose of these teams was to provide a formal setting in which inter-departmental conflicts such as the one described above between the sales manager and the research scientist could be resolved with the help of an integrator. The effective plastics firms drew on the whole range of integrative devices and needed to do so because its necessary differentiation was so high.

It is the appropriateness of the three-way relationships between the uncertainty and diversity of the environment, the degree of organizational differentiation, and the state of integration and conflict resolution achieved, which will lead to effective functioning. Inadequacy in any of these relationships was associated with lower performance. Thus, for example, the high performers in the plastics and food industry had *both* greater differentiation *and* greater integration than the low performers, since both were required. By contrast, in the low-performing container organization there was no evidence that the integrating unit it possessed was serving a useful purpose given its low level of differentiation.

Effective conflict resolution, which is the behavioural basis of integration, was found to have a pattern in which inter-unit conflict is dealt with by managers working in a problem-solving mode to face the issues and work through to the best overall solution – rather than smoothing over the issues to avoid conflict, or letting the party with the greater power force its solution on others. It was also found that in dealing with conflict effectively, the individuals primarily involved in achieving integration (whether they be superiors in the line hierarchy, or persons appointed specifically to coordinating roles) need to have their authority based not just on their formal position, but largely on their knowledge of and competence on the issues as perceived by all the groups involved, together with a balanced orientation between the parties. The power and influence to make decisions leading to the resolution of conflict must therefore be located at the points where the knowledge to reach such decisions also exists.

The Lawrence and Lorsch framework, by emphasizing that the appropriate organization structure will depend upon the environmental demands, takes a 'contingency' approach, rejecting the formulation that one particular structural form (e.g. bureaucracy, see Weber, p. 17) or one particular motivational approach (e.g. Theory Y, see McGregor, p. 167) is always best. It is the appropriateness which is the key.

Lorsch and Morse in a further study compared two manufacturing plants (one high-performing, one low-performing) with two research laboratories (similarly high and low performers). The organization structures and processes of the high-performing manufacturer in a relatively certain environment were: high formality, short time-horizon, highly directive management. The individuals working in this organization were found to have low cognitive complexity, low tolerance for ambiguity, and dependency in authority relationships. The high-performing research laboratory in a relatively uncertain environment had low formality, long time-horizons and high participation. Its members had high cognitive complexity, high tolerance for ambiguity and independence in authority relationships. Yet both organizations were effective because they were appropriately organized with appropriate members for their environmental tasks. Indeed the less effective organization in each pair did not show most of the distinctive characteristics of structure and process to the same degree. On the other hand the characteristics of the members were as clearly differentiated as in the successful organizations. These less effective organizations, it seems, could obtain the appropriate people but not organize them in the appropriate way. But equally, in other cases failure could be due to having inappropriate people even though they were appropriately organized.

The analysis of matrix organizations has been a particular concern of Davis and Lawrence. Matrix organization structures are those in which there is a multiple command system – many managers having two bosses. For example, a finance manager would have a finance director to whom he would be responsible for professional standards, and who would be concerned with his career development and promotion, and also a project director to whom he would be responsible for giving the appropriate cost accounting services that are necessary for the project and who would be concerned with his work allocation. Clearly this form of structure violates Fayol's principle of 'unity of command' (see p. 66) and its greater complexity would be the preferred structure only in certain situations. These are when (1) there are several highly salient sectors (i.e. products, markets, functions, etc.) which are simultaneously necessary for goal achievement; (2) the tasks are uncertain, complex and interdependent; and (3) there is a need to realize economies by using scarce resources effectively. In these circumstances, there is a need for complex differentiation and integration via the matrix mode.

Bibliography

Lawrence, P. R., and Lorsch, J. W., *Organization and Environment,* Harvard, 1967.

Lawrence, P. R., and Lorsch, J. W., *Developing Organizations: Diagnosis and Action,* Addison-Wesley, 1969.

Lorsch, J. W., and Morse, J. J., *Organizations and Their Members: A Contingency Approach,* Harper & Row, 1974.

Davis, S. M., and Lawrence, P. R., *Matrix,* Addison-Wesley, 1977.

Alfred D. Chandler

Alfred Chandler is Straus Professor of Business History in the Graduate School of Business Administration, Harvard University. He is an economic historian and his research work has centred on the study of business history and, in particular, administration. He has long argued that this is a much neglected area in the study of recent history. His studies of big business have been carried out with grants from a number of sources including the Alfred P. Sloan Foundation. His work has been internationally recognized, and his book *The Visible Hand* was awarded the Pulitzer Prize for History and the Bancroft Prize. Chandler has taught at a variety of universities in the United States and Europe.

All of Chandler's academic work has been concerned with the theme of the rise and role of the large-scale business enterprise during what he describes as the formative years of modern capitalism. These are the years 1850–1920. He suggests, from his many studies, that during this period a new economic institution was created, the multi-unit firm, controlled by a new class of managers operating within a new system of capitalism. These new managers had to develop strategies different from those of their entrepreneurial predecessors and be particularly innovative in creating structures to implement those strategies. The reasons for this shift are to be found in changes in demand bringing about mass markets and technological change which allowed high volume production. The new organization structures allowed the integration of mass production with mass distribution.

While Chandler's analysis is historical, he makes general points about organizational change and the relationship between strategy and structure. In particular, from his studies, Chandler is clear that the structure of an organization follows from the strategy that is adopted. The distinction between these two is crucial. *Strategy* is the determination of basic long-term goals and objectives together with the adoption of courses of action and the allocation of resources for carrying out those goals. *Structure* is the organization which is devised to administer the activities which arise from the strategies adopted. As such it involves the existence of a hierarchy, the distribution of work and lines of authority and communication. In addition, the concept of structure covers the information and data that flow along those lines.

Once an organization moves away from the small, owner-controlled enterprise towards the modern, multi-unit business enterprise then the new class of managers appears. This is important for structural developments because the salaried manager is committed to the long-term stability of the enterprise. The managerial hierarchy gives positions of power and authority and as a result becomes both a source of permanence and continued growth. As part of this process the careers of salaried managers become increasingly technical and professional.

The role of management in developing structure is central to Chandler's analysis. As he puts it, 'the visible hand of management has replaced Adam Smith's invisible hand of market forces'. The manager is both a product of, and a developer of the multi-divisional, decentralized structure which is the general product of technological change and rising demand. He becomes responsible for the administration of the enterprise, that is, coordinating, planning and appraising work, and allocating resources.

The structural arrangements of a large business enterprise have to allow for both the efficient day-to-day operations of its various units and for dealing with the long-run health of the company. The developments which follow from this involve operating with a decentralized structure to deal with day-to-day manufacturing and services, and building up a central office with functional departments to manage the long-run prospects of the company. This is all part of the process of specialization of functions as a major structural device. The key distinctions are between the general office, divisions, departments and field units. Each of these has a particular function and one of the basic reasons for the success of this type of structure is that it clearly removed from the immediate operations those executives responsible for long-term planning and appraisal. The significance of this separation is that it gives those executives the time, information and psychological commitment for long-term activities.

The introduction of this distinctive organizational structure with its unique managerial hierarchy marked the transition from a family- or finance-based capitalism to managerial capitalism. But because, in Chandler's view, structure follows strategy this transition could only occur in response to external pressures. Particularly important was the increasing volume of activity which arose in response to the new national and increasingly urban markets of the late nineteenth century. Together with this was technological change which enabled enterprises to move into high-volume production.

In the face of such pressures, enterprises could adopt either defensive or positive strategies. A *positive strategy* occurs when an enterprise actively looks for new markets and new products to serve those markets. It is organized around product diversification. A *defensive strategy* is where an enterprise acts to protect its current position. The common way of achieving this is to form a vertically integrated company by means of mergers with similar enterprises, suppliers and customers.

Both strategies lead to bigger organizations which have administrative problems. This begins a systematization of techniques for the administration of functional activities. An initial type of organization for achieving this is the centralized, functionally departmentalized structure. It enables the necessary new expert skills to be brought in but retains control by the owners. But the increase in scale of organizations involves building up capacity and enlarging the resources of men, money and materials at the disposal of an enterprise. A result of this is further and continuing growth to ensure the full use of those resources, a result which emanates from the interests of the new managers rather than the owners. Growth becomes internally as well as externally generated and then produces the really innovative structure, that of the multi-unit decentralized form.

To illustrate his points in detail and to chart the process of structural innovation, Chandler looks at the cases of four companies: Du Pont, General Motors, Standard Oil of New Jersey and Sears Roebuck. According to Chandler, the general pressures and needs facing these four companies were the same. Also in general terms, the structural outcome was very similar. But the process of diagnosing the issues and introducing the consequent administrative changes was quite different.

The particular structural innovation of Du Pont was to create autonomous divisions. The company reached the beginning of the twentieth century as a loose federation with no central administrative control. The first strategy of the younger Du Ponts was to centralize control and concentrate manufacturing activity in a few, larger plants. This was the centralized, functionally departmentalized structure. Important to the operation of the company was the development of new forms of management information and forecasting. The introduction of the multi-unit, decentralized structure came with the need to maintain growth. It was done by basing the structure on a new principle, coordinating related effort rather than like things. This innovative principle meant that different broad functional activities had to be placed in separate administrative units. To operate these units, the executives responsible were given enhanced authority. Eventually these developed into product-based units backed by a central, general office to deal with strategic issues. This left the autonomous units to get on with day-to-day operations.

The General Motors case underlines the need for structure to follow strategy. Durant, the founder of General Motors, went for a volume strategy with many operating units in a loose federation. There was a crisis in 1920 due to a lack of overall control. The response of Sloan (p. 138) was to create a general office to be responsible for broad policies and objectives and to coordinate effort. A line-and-staff structure was developed, allowing the product divisions to ensure good use of resources and a proper product flow, with the headquarters staff appraising divisional performance and plans. The new structure took five years to put in place.

As with General Motors, Standard Oil of New Jersey was, for Chandler, a case of initial failure to adjust structure to strategy. The channels of authority and communication were insufficiently defined within a partly federated, partly consolidated company. As a result there was a series of crises over inventories and over-production during the 1920s which led to *ad hoc* responses. The initial development was to build up a central office for resource allocation and coordination. A second stage was to set up a decentralized divisional structure. According to Chandler, the response in Standard Oil was slower and more tentative than in Du Pont or General Motors partly because the problems were more difficult and partly because of a general lack of concern with organizational problems.

During the 1920s and 1930s, Sears Roebuck underwent the same process in its own particular way, partly planned and partly unplanned. The initial defensive strategy of vertical integration produced a centralized, functionally departmentalized structure. Continued growth produced the pressure for decentralized, regional organization and for sorting out the relationships between operating units and functional departments.

For Chandler, both his case studies and his broader work illustrate a number of general points about structural development and organizational innovation. The first is that the market and technological pressures of an urban, industrial society push enterprises in the same structural direction, but the actual process of innovation can be quite different. In this process it is important to distinguish between an adaptive response and a creative innovation. An *adaptive response* is a structural change which stays within the range of current custom and practice as was the case with functional departments and a central office. A *creative innovation* goes beyond existing practice and procedures, developing decentralized field units for example. The general adoption of a line-and-staff departmental structure meant that delegation of authority and responsibility to field units was possible.

From this process, says Chandler, there arises a new economic function in society, that of administrative coordination and control. To carry out that function, a new sub-species of economic man is created, the salaried manager. In carrying out the function the modern business enterprise is produced, with its two specific characteristics – the existence of many distinct operating units and their management by a hierarchy of salaried executives.

Bibliography

Chandler, A. D., *Strategy and Structure,* MIT Press, 1962.
Chandler, A. D., *The Visible Hand: The Managerial Revolution in American Business,* Harvard University Press, 1977.

Oliver E. Williamson

Oliver Williamson, an American economist, began his working life as a project engineer in US government service, but soon moved into academic life taking degrees at the universities of Stanford and Carnegie-Mellon. His career took him through leading American universities to become Professor in the Department of Economics at the University of Pennsylvania.

Williamson probes beneath the usual questions about what organizations are like and how their members behave to ask why they are there at all. Why organizations? His answer is because they lower the cost of transactions. He sees society as a network of transactions – contracts in the widest sense of that term – and suggests that a 'transactional paradigm' will yield the reasons for organizations. These reasons are not size – that is, the economies of scale which have been supposed to explain large organizations – nor large-scale technologies, but the information cost of transactions. Size and technology are important not in themselves but because of the demands they make for information.

Each of the multitude of recurrent transactions which take place in a society can be conducted either in a market or within an organization. Which mode of transacting is used depends upon the information available and the costs to the transacting parties of adding to that information should they require more. So as the requirements for information change, transactions may be conducted more in markets, or more and more within organizations. The trend has been for more transactions to be gathered within the boundaries of organizations, and Williamson's discussion is primarily about change in that direction. That is because he has been concerned mainly with societies moving that way, but if the starting point were a society in which central planning and non-market transactions predominated, the analysis could as appropriately deal with the shifting of transactions from within organizations out to markets. Analysis of transaction costs can answer 'why not organizations?' as well as 'why organizations?'

Williamson's point of view joins market economics to organization theory in a form of institutional economics. He looks forward to the possibility that measures of market structure will eventually combine with measures of the internal structure of organizations (see Derek Pugh and the Aston Group, p. 37).

Markets and *hierarchies* are alternatives for conducting transactions. So transactions are brought within the hierarchical structures of organizations when the market mode is no longer efficient. For example, mergers or takeovers bring into a single organization contracting parties whose transactions will then be regulated by the internal rules of a hierarchy and not by the rules of a market. Or organizations are set up to transact within themselves business that might alternatively have been done by separate parties contracting between themselves in market terms.

Which mode is adopted depends upon the degree of *information impactedness*. This exists when the 'true underlying circumstances' of a transaction are known to one or more parties but not to others. Where there is less than complete trust between the parties, those who lack information could only obtain parity by incurring costs, which may be high, even prohibitive. Thus a buyer who is offered supplies may be unsure whether the quality will be what is required, whether delivery is likely to be on time, or how far the proposed price is more than need be paid. This may be because no one, not even the seller, has adequate information on these matters; or it may be that even if information is available, the buyer cannot trust it because the seller will have interpreted it to favour the selling vantage point.

A market is the most efficacious mode of conducting transactions when all necessary information is conveyed between parties by a price, and this single item of information is sufficient. Transactions are better brought within a hierarchy when much more must be known, much less is certain, and there may be 'quasi-moral' elements, for the hierarchy brings the inadequately informed parties to a transaction together under some degree of control. Two firms which have had a market relationship and then merge will gain access to the other's information and are better able to foresee what the other will do.

Williamson sees information impactedness as a 'derivative condition', itself derived from two pairs of factors. Human factors are paired with environmental factors: human *bounded rationality* with environmental *uncertainty/complexity*, and human *opportunism* with the *number of parties* in the environment. The joining of these pairs of factors sets the conditions which give rise to greater or lesser information impactedness and thence to either markets or hierarchies.

Williamson takes the idea of bounded rationality from Simon (see p. 104). Full rationality in human action is unattainable because the capacity of the mind for formulating and solving complex problems is bounded by neurophysiological limits (mental capacity is not infinite), and the ability of individuals to transmit what they know or feel is bounded by the limits of language (words fail them). So each party to a transaction operates within its own bounded rationality.

The bounds of that rationality are reached under conditions of uncertainty or complexity. If there were both full rationality and complete certainty then all contingent actions could be specified at the outset. The parties would comprehend everything and know exactly what to do. An entire 'decision tree' of alternative decisions in various circumstances could be written out. But given bounded rationality together with uncertainty or complexity, this is impossible (complexity is equivalent to uncertainty, for even if the individual ingredients of a highly complex problem are each certain, their sheer number defies computation and results in uncertainty). Hence bounded rationality, confronted with uncertainty-complexity, results in information impactedness.

The second human characteristic, opportunism, is the manipulation of information to self-advantage. It is guile, the presentation of information in a favourable form, misrepresentation, empty threats or promises. Even with a detailed agreement corners can be cut in ways which are difficult for others to discern. Yet this of itself is not sufficient for information impactedness. There must also be small numbers of parties in the transaction situation.

Large numbers would frustrate opportunistic inclinations, because alternative parties, whose behaviour is less opportunistic, can be found with whom to transact. Small numbers encourage opportunistic representations and haggling. Further, what may once have been, and still appears to be, a large numbers situation may in effect be only a small numbers situation, for whoever concluded an earlier contract then has the advantage over competitors of special know-how when the contract comes up for renewal.

Conditions change. Uncertainty may diminish. Market growth may support larger numbers. So the conditions of the pairs of factors which give rise to either market transactions or organizational transactions may no longer hold. That mode then fails, meaning that the economic friction associated with it in the form of information costs reaches an uneconomic level.

Transactions will be shifted out of a market and into the hierarchy of a firm, or other form of organization, when information impactedness is high, that is when the uncertainties and distrust inherent in transactions become too great for prices to be acceptably determined. At this point the advantages of a hierarchy become the greater. First, it extends the bounds on rationality. Though the rationalities of each of the parties within an organization are still restricted, specialization enables each to deal with a part of the overall problem that is small enough to be comprehended, the results of the work of them all being brought together by specialized decision makers at the apex. More information is exchanged or can be required to be handed over. Common numbering and coding systems and occupational jargon cut down communication costs. Second, sub-sections of an organization can each attend to a given aspect of the uncertainty-complexity of a situation so making manageable a problem which would in total be too uncertain-complex. Aspects can be attended to as the situation unfolds, rather than all at once, and decisions which might otherwise be too complex can be split down into smaller sequential steps (see Lindblom, p. 116). Third, a hierarchy curbs opportunism. Pay, promotion, and control techniques ensure that the parties work in some degree towards common goals. Confidence may not be complete but it is greater. Parties cannot use their gains entirely for their own ends, and what they do can be more effectively checked and audited. Should disputes arise, superior hierarchical levels can decide them. Fourth, where there are small numbers, a situation which opportunistic parties are inclined to take advantage of, the hierarchy can overrule bargaining.

In general then, hierarchy more nearly approaches parity of

information, and in particular provides for quasi-moral and recipro-cal obligations over and above strictly economic ones.

What then stops hierarchies taking over more and more trans-actions indefinitely? The limits begin to appear as firms grow larger and as vertical integration between firms extends. Costs then rise to a level at which the marginal costs of administering the incre-mental transaction begin to exceed those of completing transactions through a market. The goals of groups or sub-sections within an organization start to outweigh the common aims, the proliferation of specialists in control systems to combat this tendency becomes more and more expensive, sunk costs encourage the persistence of existing ways of doing things even if they would not now be done that way, were they to be started afresh, and communication is increasingly distorted. Leaders become more distant from those they lead – 'bureaucratic insularity' – and cooperation between those at lower levels becomes perfunctory rather than wholehearted. Coordination and common purpose lapse.

These costs rise in the unitary form of hierarchy, the single large organization, as it endeavours to control the transactions within it. However, the stage at which organizational transactions again become the most costly can be staved off by the adoption of a multi-divisional structure. A classic example was General Motors in the USA (see Sloan, p. 138, Chandler, p. 53). The organization is sub-divided into a number of quasi-autonomous sub-organizations or operating divisions. Each division is largely self-sufficient with its own functional departments (e.g. production, sales, finance, personnel, etc.) and is responsible for specific products or, alterna-tively, specific geographic areas. To be effective, this form of organization requires a general overall management which concen-trates on monitoring the performance of the constituent divisions and on strategic planning. Management can use the multi-divisional structure as a miniature capital market in which funds are moved into the most profitable uses more effectively than by the external capital market, because internally there is more complete information about the firm than parties in the external capital market have about comparative investment opportunities. But if general management gets involved in the day-to-day operation of the divisions, information costs will again be forced up until market transactions become more attractive.

For ultimately it is the relative cost of overcoming information impactedness that determines whether the transactions in a society are conducted through markets or within organizations.

Bibliography

Williamson, O. E., *Markets and Hierarchies: Analysis and Antitrust Implications — A Study in the Economics of Internal Organization,* Free Press and Collier Macmillan, 1975.

2 · *The Functioning of Organizations*

To manage is to forecast and plan, to organize, to command, to coordinate
and to control.

Henri Fayol

A cooperative system is incessantly dynamic, a process of continual re-
adjustment to physical, biological and social environments as a whole.

Chester I. Barnard

Most organizations most of the time cannot rely on their participants to
carry out their assignments voluntarily.

Amitai Etzioni

Hierarchy is divisive, it creates resentment, hostility and opposition ...
Paradoxically, through participation management increases its control by
giving up some of its authority.

Arnold S. Tannenbaum

Only organizations based on the redundancy of functions (as opposed to
the redundancy of parts) have the flexibility and innovative potential to
give the possibility of adaptation to a rapid change rate, increasing complexity and environmental uncertainty.

E. L. Trist

By beginning from, and attempting to make sense of, the definitions of the
situation held by the actors, the Action perspective provides a means of
understanding the range of reactions to apparently 'identical' social
situations.

David Silverman

Work expands so as to fill the time available for its completion.

C. Northcote Parkinson

Accepting the likelihood of a number of types of organization, as writers on the structure of organizations suggest, is it feasible to think of analysing their activities? Is it possible to break down into categories what an organization does? Several theoretical schemes have been proposed for this purpose, applicable either to industrial enterprises or, more widely, to all organizations. Their originators have the view that some common classification is essential to bring order into the thoughts of those who try to understand organizations.

Attempts to develop unified analyses of organizational functioning, offering differing but widely applicable concepts, have been offered by both managers and academics. Two top managers, the Frenchman Henri Fayol and the American Chester I. Barnard have put forward analyses based on their long experience and personal insight. Amitai Etzioni examines the basis on which organizations obtain the 'compliance' of their members, and Arnold Tannenbaum analyses the nature of control in organizations.

Eric Trist and his colleagues at the Tavistock Institute demonstrate the utility of regarding organizations as functioning open 'socio-technical' systems, while in contrast David Silverman argues that the 'Action Frame of Reference' contributes more to our understanding of organizational functioning.

Finally, C. Northcote Parkinson amusingly but insightfully analyses certain practices of which organizations must beware if they are to function efficiently.

Henri Fayol

Henri Fayol (1841–1925) was a mining engineer by training. A Frenchman, he spent his working life with the French mining and metallurgical combine Commentry-Fourchamboult-Decazeville, first as an engineer but from his early thirties onwards in general management. From 1888 to 1918 he was Managing Director.

Fayol is among those who have achieved fame for ideas made known very late in life. He was in his seventies before he published them in a form which came to be widely read. He had written technical articles on mining engineering and a couple of preliminary papers on administration, but it was in 1916 that the *Bulletin de la Société de l'Industrie Minerale* printed Fayol's *Administration Industrielle et Générale – Prévoyance, Organisation, Commandement, Coordination, Contrôle*. He is also among those whose reputation rests on a single short publication still frequently reprinted as a book; his other writings are little known.

The English version appears as *General and Industrial Management*, translated by Constance Storrs and first issued in 1949. There has been some debate over this rendering of the title of the work, and in particular of expressing the French word '*administration*' by the term 'management'. It is argued that this could simply imply that Fayol is concerned only with industrial management, whereas his own preface claims that: 'Management plays a very important part in the government of undertakings; of all undertakings, large or small, industrial, commercial, political, religious or any other.' Indeed, in his last years he studied the problems of State public services and lectured at the École Supérieure de la Guerre. So it can be accepted that his intention was to initiate a theoretical analysis appropriate to a wide range of organizations.

Fayol suggests that: 'All activities to which industrial undertakings give rise can be divided into the following six groups:

1. Technical activities (production, manufacture, adaptation).
2. Commercial activities (buying, selling, exchange).

3. Financial activities (search for and optimum use of capital).
4. Security activities (protection of property and persons).
5. Accounting activities (stocktaking, balance sheet, costs, statistics).
6. Managerial activities (planning, organization, command, coordination, control).

Be the undertaking simple or complex, big or small, these six groups of activities or essential functions are always present.'

Most of these six groups of activities will be present in most jobs, but in varying measure, with the managerial element in particular being greatest in senior jobs and least or absent in direct production or lower clerical tasks. Managerial activities are specially emphasized as being universal to organizations. But it is a commonplace to ask: What is management? Is it anything that can be identified and stand on its own, or is it a word, a label, that has no substance?

Fayol's answer was unique at the time. The core of his contribution is his definition of management as comprising five elements:

1. To forecast and plan (in the French, *prévoyance*): 'examining the future and drawing up the plan of action'.
2. To organize: 'building up the structure, material and human, of the undertaking'.
3. To command: 'maintaining activity among the personnel'.
4. To coordinate: 'binding together, unifying and harmonizing all activity and effort'.
5. To control: 'seeing that everything occurs in conformity with established rule and expressed command'.

For Fayol, managing means looking ahead, which makes the process of *forecasting and planning* a central business activity. Management must 'assess the future and make provision for it'. To function adequately a business organization needs a plan which has the characteristics of 'unity, continuity, flexibility and precision'. The problems of planning which management must overcome are: making sure that the objectives of each part of the organization are securely welded together (unity); using both short- and long-term forecasting (continuity); being able to adapt the plan in the light of changing circumstances (flexibility); and attempting to accurately predict courses of action (precision). The essence of planning is to allow the optimum use of resources. Interestingly, Fayol in 1916 argued the necessity of a national plan for France, to be produced by the government.

To *organize* is 'building up the structure, material and human, of the undertaking'. The task of management is to build up an organization which will allow the basic activities to be carried out in an optimal manner. Central to this is a structure in which plans are efficiently prepared and carried out. There must be unity of command and direction, clear definition of responsibilities, precise decision-making backed up by an efficient system for selecting and training managers.

Fayol's third element comes logically after the first two. An organization must start with a plan, a definition of its goals. It then must produce an organization structure appropriate to the achievement of those goals. Third, the organization must be put in motion, which is *command*, maintaining activity among the personnel. Through his ability to command, the manager obtains the best possible performance from his subordinates. This he does through example, knowledge of the business, knowledge of his subordinates, continuous contact with his staff, and by maintaining a broad view of his function. In this way he maintains a high level of activity by instilling a sense of mission.

Command refers to the relationship between a manager and the subordinates in his immediate task area. But organizations have a variety of tasks to perform, so *coordination* is necessary 'binding together, unifying and harmonizing all activity and effort'. Essentially this is making sure that one department's efforts are coincident with the efforts of other departments, and keeping all activities in perspective with regard to the overall aims of the organization. This can only be attained by a constant circulation of information and regular meetings of management.

Finally there is *control*, logically the final element which checks that the other four elements are in fact performing properly: 'seeing that everything occurs in conformity with established rule and expressed command.' To be effective, control must operate quickly and there must be a system of sanctions. The best way to ensure this is to separate all functions concerned with inspection from the operation departments whose work they inspect. Fayol believed in independent, impartial staff departments.

Fayol uses this classification to divide up his chapters on how to administer or manage. It is probable that when he wrote of *'une doctrine administrative'* he had in mind not only the above theory but the addition of experience to theoretical analysis to form a doctrine of good management. He summarizes the lessons of his own experience in a number of General Principles of Management. These are his own rules and he does not assume they are necessarily of universal application nor that they have any great permanence. None the less, most have become part of managerial know-how and many are regarded as fundamental tenets. Fayol outlines the following fourteen principles:

1. Division of work: specialization allows the individual to build up expertise and thereby be more productive.
2. Authority: the right to issue commands, along with which must go the equivalent responsibility for its exercise.
3. Discipline: which is two-sided, for employees only obey orders if management play their part by providing good leadership.
4. Unity of command: in contrast to F. W. Taylor's functional authority (see p. 136), Fayol was quite clear that each man should have only one boss with no other conflicting lines of command. On this issue history has favoured Fayol, for his principle has found most adherents among managers.
5. Unity of direction: people engaged in the same kind of activities must have the same objectives in a single plan.
6. Subordination of individual interest to general interest: management must see that the goals of the firm are always paramount.
7. Remuneration: payment is an important motivator although, by analysing a number of different possibilities, Fayol points out that there is no such thing as a perfect system.
8. Centralization or decentralization: again this is a matter of degree depending on the condition of the business and the quality of its personnel.
9. Scalar chain: a hierarchy is necessary for unity of direction but lateral communication is also fundamental as long as superiors know that such communication is taking place.
10. Order: both material order and social order are necessary. The former minimizes lost time and useless handling of materials. The latter is achieved through organization and selection.

11. Equity: in running a business, a 'combination of kindliness and justice' is needed in treating employees if equity is to be achieved.

12. Stability of tenure: this is essential due to the time and expense involved in training good management. Fayol believes that successful businesses tend to have more stable managerial personnel.

13. Initiative: allowing all personnel to show their initiative in some way is a source of strength for the organization even though it may well involve a sacrifice of 'personal vanity' on the part of many managers.

14. *Esprit de corps*: management must foster the morale of its employees and, to quote Fayol, 'real talent is needed to coordinate effort, encourage keenness, use each man's abilities, and reward each one's merit without arousing possible jealousies and disturbing harmonious relations.'

But Fayol's pride of place in this field is due not so much to his principles of how to manage, enduring though these are, as to his definition of what management is. He is the earliest known proponent of a theoretical analysis of managerial activities – an analysis which has withstood almost a half-century of critical discussion. There can have been few writers since who have not been influenced by it; and his five elements have provided a system of concepts with which managers may clarify their thinking about what it is they have to do.

Bibliography

Fayol, H., *General and Industrial Management,* London: Pitman, 1949. Translated by Constance Storrs from the original *Administration Industrielle et Générale,* 1916.

Chester I. Barnard

Chester I. Barnard (1886–1961) was for many years President of the New Jersey Bell Telephone Company. On two occasions he was seconded for duty as State Director of the New Jersey Relief Administration, a government organization which allowed him many opportunities for contrasting the functioning of an established organization with one created *ad hoc* under conditions of stress. During the Second World War he developed and managed the United Service Organizations, Inc. As a practising top manager he had a continuing interest in describing organizational activities and the social and personal relationships between the people involved. This culminated in his classic book *The Functions of the Executive*, first published in 1938. His selected papers have also been published under the title *Organization and Management*.

Barnard begins his analysis from the premise that individuals must cooperate. This is because a human being has only limited power of choice, for he is confined partly by the situation in which he acts and partly by the biological restrictions of his nature. The most effective method of overcoming these limitations is cooperative social action. This requires that he adopt a group, or non-personal, purpose and take into consideration the processes of interaction. The persistence of cooperation depends on its effectiveness in accomplishing the cooperative purpose, and its efficiency in satisfying the individual's motives.

A formal organization for Barnard is a 'system of consciously coordinated activities or forces of two or more persons'. This definition, and the analysis based on it, can be applied to all forms of organization: the state, the church, the factory, the family. An organization comes into being when '(i) there are persons able to communicate with each other (ii) who are willing to contribute action (iii) to accomplish a common purpose'. Willingness to *contribute action* in this context means the surrender of the control of personal conduct in order to achieve coordination. Clearly the commitment of particular persons to do this will vary from maximum willingness through a neutral point to opposition or hatred. Indeed Barnard maintains that, in modern society, the majority of possible contributors to any given organization will lie on the negative side in their commitment. Equally important, the commitment of any individual will fluctuate, and thus the total willingness of all contributors to cooperate in any formal system is unstable – a fact which is evident from the history of all such organizations. Willingness to cooperate is the result of the satisfactions or dissatisfactions obtained, and all organizations depend upon the essentially subjective assessment of these made by the members.

All organizations have a *purpose*, but this does not produce cooperative activity unless it is accepted by the members. A purpose thus has both a cooperative and a subjective aspect. The subjective aspect is not the meaning of the purpose to the individual but rather what the individual thinks it means to the organization as a whole. Thus a man will carry out a job he dislikes if he accepts it as relevant to the aim of the whole organization and to his part in it. The essential basis for cooperative action is a cooperative purpose which is *believed* by the contributors to be that of the organization. 'The inculcation of belief in the real existence of a common purpose is an essential executive function.' The continuance of an organization depends on its ability to carry out its purpose, but there is the paradox that it destroys itself by accomplishing its objectives, as is shown by the large number of successful organizations which disappear through failure to renew them. Continuing organizations require the repeated adoption of new purposes. This process is often concealed by stating a generalized purpose which appears not to change, e.g. giving a service, making motor-cars. But the real purpose is not 'service' as an abstraction, but specific acts of service; not making motor-cars in general, but making specific motor-cars from day to day.

The other essential for a formal organization is *communication*, linking the common purpose with those willing to cooperate in it. Communication is necessary to translate purpose into action. The methods of communication are firstly language – oral and written – and, secondly, 'observational feeling'. This is the ability to understand, without words, not merely the situation but also the intention. It results from special experience and training and continuity in association, which leads the members of the organization to develop common perceptions and reactions to particular situations.

Large organizations are made up of numbers of basic units. These units are small – from two to fifteen persons – and are limited in their growth by the limitations of intercommunication. The size of a unit depends on the complexity of the purpose and the technological conditions for action, the difficulty of the communication process, the extent to which communication is necessary, and the complexity of the personal relationships involved. These last increase with great rapidity as the number of persons in the unit group increases. Moreover, groups are related to each other. As the number of possible groups increases, the complexity of group relationships increases in greater ratio.

Interactions between persons which are based on personal rather than joint or common purposes will, because of their repetitive character, become systematic and organized. This will be the informal organization, which will have an important effect on the thought and action of the members. Barnard envisages a continual interaction between formal and informal organization. An informal organization to be effective – particularly if it is of any size – must give rise to formal organization, which makes explicit many of its attitudes and institutions. Formal organizations once established must create, if they are to operate effectively, informal organizations as a means of communication and cohesion and as a way of protecting the integrity of the individual against domination by the formal organization. This last function may seem to operate against the aims of the formal organization, but it is in fact vital to it. For it is by giving the individual a sphere where he is able to exercise personal choice and not have his decisions dominated by the impersonal objectives of the formal organization, that the personality of the individual is safeguarded and his continuing effective contribution to the formal organization made more likely.

On the basis of his analysis of organizational functioning, Barnard describes the functions of the executive. The members of the executive organization are contributors to two units in a complex organization – a basic working unit and an executive unit. Thus a foreman is regarded as a member of a shop group as well as of the department management group; an army captain is a member of his company and of the 'regimental organization'. Under such conditions a single action is an activity of two different unit organizations. It is this simultaneous contribution which makes the complex organization into an organic whole.

It is important to recognize that not all work carried out by the executive is executive work. Executive work is 'the specialized work of *maintaining* the organization in operation' and consists of three tasks:

1. The maintenance of organizational communication.
2. The securing of essential services from individuals.
3. The formulation of purpose and objectives.

The task of *communication* has two phases: the first is the definition of organizational positions – the 'scheme of organization'. This requires organization charts, specification of duties, and the like. It represents a coordination of the work to be done. But the scheme of organization is of little value without the personnel to fill the positions. The second phase of the task of communication is the recruiting of contributors who have the appropriate qualifications. But both phases are dependent on each other. 'Men are neither good nor bad but only good or bad in this or that position'; and often the scheme of organization has to be changed to take account of the men available. The informal executive organization has the function of expanding the means of communication and thus reducing the need for formal decisions. The issuing of formal decisions, except for routine matters and for emergencies, is unnecessary with a good informal organization. In this situation, a formal order is the recognition that agreement has been obtained on the decision by informal means. It is part of the art of leadership to eschew conflict in formal order-giving by issuing only those formal orders which are acceptable. Disagreements must be dealt with by informal means.

The task of *securing the essential services* from individuals has two main divisions: bringing persons into cooperative relationship with the organization, and eliciting the services of such people. Both are achieved by maintaining morale, and by maintaining schemes of incentives, deterrents, supervision and control, and education and training.

The third executive task is the *formulation of the purposes* of the organization. The critical aspect here is 'the assignment of responsibility – the delegation of objective authority'. Responsibility for abstract long-term decisions on purpose lies with the executive organization, but responsibility for action remains at the base. The definition of purpose in particular situations is a widely distributed function; hence there is a need to indoctrinate those at the lower levels with general purposes and major decisions, if the organization is to be a cohesive organic whole.

As a practising manager in industry and in public service Barnard has combined a thorough knowledge of the workings of organization with a wide reading of sociology. As a result his work has had a great impact on the thinking both of managers and of academics.

Bibliography

Barnard, C. I., *The Functions of the Executive,* Harvard University Press, 1938.

Barnard, C. I., *Organization and Management,* Harvard University Press, 1948.

Amitai Etzioni

Amitai Etzioni is a sociologist at Columbia University, New York, having previously worked at the Hebrew University, Jerusalem, and the Berkeley campus of the University of California. He is currently working in the area of conflict and peace research, something which grew out of his organizational interests. His concern with fundamental sociological problems led him to examine organizations as promising research sites for their solution.

In his work he starts from the problem of social order, asking the question of why organizations, or other social entities, keep going. This is the problem of social control which has interested social philosophers since the days of Plato and which was put in its most pristine form by Hobbes. It is similar to the concern of Weber (p. 13), and for Etzioni too the question to be answered is 'why do people in organizations conform to the orders given to them and follow the standards of behaviour laid down for them?' This problem occurs in all social organizations from the family to the nation state, but Etzioni sees it as being particularly crucial in formal organizations. This is because organizations are designed as instruments. When one is formed, whether it be in government, business, education or recreation, it has a specific reason for existing, a goal or purpose; 'natural' social systems such as the family, or a community, are much more diverse in what they do and it is difficult to think of them having goals. But because organizations have this characteristic of attempting to reach a goal, it becomes important to 'measure' how well they are doing. The result is an emphasis on performance.

Organizations continuously review their performance and will change their practices in the light of this. Organizations therefore face special problems of controlling the behaviour of their members, because they must make sure that behaviour is in line with the requirements of performance.

Etzioni starts from the proposition that organizations, like other social units, require compliance from their members. Because of their intensive concern with performance (and also in the modern world, their size), organizations cannot rely on compliance coming essentially from the fact that members are completely committed to the aims of the organization. Also they cannot rely on an informal control system based on one individual influencing another such as occurs in the family. Organizations have formal systems for controlling what goes on in them; they have rewards and penalties of a clear and specific kind to ensure compliance from their members.

Compliance in any organization is two sided. On the one hand it consists of the control structures that are employed: the organizational power and authority structure which attempts to ensure that obedience is obtained. This Etzioni calls the structural aspect since it is concerned with the formal organizational system and the kind of power that the organization uses to enforce compliance. As organizations cannot completely rely on their members to carry out orders perfectly, it is necessary to have a hierarchy of authority, to have supervisors: it is necessary to have job descriptions and specified procedures for doing things; it is necessary to have a division of labour. All of these are attempts to make the organization less dependent on the whims of individuals by controlling behaviour. The organization exercises its power by these bureaucratic means.

The second aspect of compliance is based on the extent to which members of the organization are committed to its aims and purposes. This is the motivational aspect and is expressed in the kind of involvement that the individual has with the organization that he belongs to. The more intensely an individual is involved in the organization the more likely he is to work towards the realization of its goals. Etzioni argues that the more employees are committed, the less formal control mechanisms are needed. These two aspects of compliance are then used to produce a typology of organizations.

Etzioni outlines three kinds of power according to which organizations can be classified. The classification is based on the different means used to ensure that members comply. He distinguishes between coercive power, remunerative or utilitarian power, and normative or identitive power. They are based on physical, material and symbolic means respectively.

Coercive power rests essentially on the (possible) application of physical force to make sure that members of an organization comply with orders. Thus, the ability to inflict physical pain or to cause death for non-compliance is the use of this kind of power. Examples of organizations using physical means to different degrees are concentration camps and custodial mental hospitals.

Remunerative or utilitarian power rests on the manipulation of material resources. The organizational member's compliance is enforced because the organization controls materials, such as money, which the member desires. Thus, a system of rewards based on wages and salaries constitutes this kind of power. Business organizations are typically based on remunerative control.

Normative or identitive power comes from the manipulation and allocation of symbols. Examples of pure symbols are love, affection, prestige which can be used to extract compliance from others. Etzioni suggests that alternative, and perhaps more eloquent names would be persuasive or suggestive power. He sees this kind of power as most often found in religious organizations, universities, voluntary associations.

These are ideas which are useful for making broad comparative analyses of organizations based on predominant characteristics. But not all organizations with the same general objectives have similar control structures. Etzioni suggests that labour unions can be based on any of the three; 'underworld' unions controlled by mobsters relying on coercion; 'business' unions offering members wage increases and better working conditions are essentially remunerative; and 'political' unions, centred on ideologies, rely on normative power. Most organizations attempt to employ all three kinds of power, but will usually emphasize one kind of power and rely less on the other two. Often different means of control are emphasized for different participants in the organization. Members at the bottom of the organization are often more likely to be subject to coercive measures, whereas higher participants are more likely to be subject to normative power.

As with power, Etzioni suggests three kinds of involvement. The classification is based on a dimension of low to high involvement, and the types are labelled alienative, calculative, and moral. In essence, involvement in an organization can run from highly intensive negative feelings to highly positive feelings with mildly negative and mildly positive in between.

Alienative involvement is the intensely negative end, and denotes

dissociation from the organization by the member. Convicts and prisoners of war are usually alienated from the organizations of which they are members. With calculative involvement the member's relationship to the organization has little intensity and thus can be either positive or negative in a mild way. This is typical of business relationships. Finally, moral involvement denotes a positive and favourable view of the organization which is very intense. It is found in the highly committed church member, the loyal party member, etc.

When examined together, the three kinds of power and the three kinds of involvement generate nine types of compliance relationship in the organization:

Kinds of power	Kinds of involvement		
	Alienative	Calculative	Moral
Coercive	1	2	3
Remunerative	4	5	6
Normative	7	8	9

Etzioni argues that a particular kind of power and a particular kind of involvement usually go together; thus the most common forms of compliance found in organizations are 1, 5 and 9. Coercive power produces alienative involvement, and vice versa; remunerative power and calculative involvement will be found together; and similarly normative power and moral involvement are congruent with one another.

Organizations which represent these three empirically dominant types are a prison with an emphasis on custody rather than rehabilitation, a factory, and a church respectively. The other six possibilities are incongruent in the sense that the power system does not fit the involvement of the members. The result will be strain and a shift in one of the bases of compliance. Etzioni suggests that organizations which have congruent compliance structures will be more effective than those which suffer the strain and tension of incongruent systems. This argues that business organizations function most effectively when they use remuneration rather than coercion or symbols as the basis of control. They need a system which is subject to ease of measurement and which can be clearly related to performance. Coercion (such as threats of dismissal) and normative control (such as appeals to loyalty) can only be used secondarily.

However, it should always be remembered that there are many outside factors which affect the kind of control structure that an organization can have. In the kinds of societies which produce many complex organizations the state monopolizes the use of force; and indeed we find that it is state-run institutions, such as prisons, which use coercive power. Other organizations, e.g. business, are not allowed to. Similarly, general market conditions such as the extent of competition, or the presence of a labour pool, will affect the extent to which the utilitarian control used by a business firm will veer towards the coercive or normative end of the spectrum. Also, the beliefs that the participants bring to the organizations of which they are members, and their personality makeups, will affect the degree to which they recognize particular kinds of control as legitimate. Etzioni points out the differences in response between the USA of today and of two generations ago that would result from the same exercise in coercive power – for example, a teacher slapping a pupil. The changing belief system means that organizations have to change their compliance structures.

Overall, Etzioni is interested in laying the base for a wide-scale comparative analysis of organizations. As such he produces a conceptual framework which is applicable to all organizations and which emphasizes similarities and differences between organizations in different institutional areas.

Bibliography

Etzioni, A., *A Comparative Analysis of Complex Organizations,* Free Press, 1961.

Etzioni, A., *Modern Organizations,* Prentice-Hall, 1964.

Etzioni, A., 'Organizational control structure', in J. G. March (ed.), *Handbook of Organizations,* Rand McNally, 1965.

Arnold S. Tannenbaum

Arnold Tannenbaum did not begin as the social psychologist he later became. His first degree was in electrical engineering from Purdue University. He went on to take his Ph.D. at Syracuse University, and to join the staff of one of the leading and longest established American social science institutes, the Institute for Social Research not far from Detroit, where he has worked ever since as researcher, teacher and consultant. He is both a Program Director in the Institute's Survey Research Center and Professor in the Department of Psychology at the University of Michigan.

In the small text he published in 1966, Tannenbaum set out clearly the view of organizational functioning that has shaped his work for many years. 'Hierarchy is divisive, it creates resentment, hostility and opposition. Participation reduces disaffection and increases the identification of members with the organization.' What is more: 'Paradoxically, through participation, management increases its control by giving up some of its authority.'

Early in his research career, Tannenbaum found that in trade unions the more effective and active local branches had both more influential officers and more influential members, at first sight an impossibility. An impossibility, that is, if control of an organization was thought of as a given quantity, something to be divided so that if someone had more then someone else had less; but not impossible if control of an organization was expandable so that everyone could have more. It is this possibility that shapes Tannenbaum's view of what organizations can be.

His work has focused on control, for organizations are means whereby the behaviour of large numbers of individuals is controlled. That is, people have to work together more or less as they are intended to if the aims of the organizations are to be achieved, whether that organization is a trade union, a firm, a welfare agency, a cooperative or an Israeli kibbutz, a financial institution, a brokerage firm, or a branch of the American League of Women Voters – all examples of organizations which Tannenbaum and his colleagues or others following their lead have studied. Control is any process by which a person or group of persons determines (i.e. 'intentionally affects') the behaviour of another person or group, in other words, causes someone else to do what they want them to do. In an organization this may be by orders or by persuasion, by threats or by promises, through written communications or through discussion, even indirectly by fixing the speed of a machine that someone else must keep up with or by programming a computer to produce information they must deal with – or by any other means having such an effect.

The way of representing control used in studies by Tannenbaum and his colleagues over many years is to ask members of organizations how much influence they and others have. They are asked a question worded typically as follows: 'How much say or influence does each of the following groups have over what goes on (in the organization)?' The groups referred to are hierarchical echelons such as managers, supervisors, and workers; the groupings can be varied as appropriate. This simple question is capable of yielding a great amount of information since even with only three groups – managers, supervisors and workers – those in each group can rate the influence of both the other two groups and of themselves, so that a large number of cross-checking ratings are obtained. If four, five or six groupings are used the information is greater again. The wording of the question can also be varied to refer more specifically to the influence over what others do or over policy, for example.

Members of organizations respond to the question by ticking one of five categories for each group, in the form:

	Little or no influence	Some influence	Quite a bit of influence	A great deal of influence	A very great deal of influence
Managers	—	—	—	—	—
Supervisors	—	—	—	—	—
Workers	—	—	—	—	—

The degrees of influence are scored from one to five so that a tick under 'Little' scores one, a tick under 'Some' scores two, and so on with 'A very great deal' scoring five.

Responding to such a question in this way gives a representation of how actual influence is perceived by those involved. A second and equally large amount of information is obtained by asking the same question again but with the word 'does' replaced by 'should'. This gives preferred or ideal influence.

The impact of Tannenbaum's work, and its interpretation, are heightened by the way in which the results can be portrayed. They can be plotted on what are called control graphs. Various different averagings of scores can be plotted, but usually the influence ratings given to each group by all the others and by itself are added and its mean score is calculated. In the example above, this would give a mean score out of five for managers, another for supervisors, and another for workers, which could then be plotted on a control graph in which the three hierarchical groups were placed evenly along the lateral axis in hierarchical order. A simplified but not unrepresentative hypothetical result might look like the graph below.

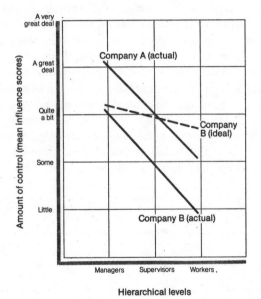

The lines are drawn through the three graph points for the mean scores for each group (managers, workers, supervisors) on the vertical control (influence score) axis.

The immediate visual impact of a control graph is from the *slope* of the lines, its most obvious if not necessarily most significant feature. In the graph, the two solid lines represent the actual (as against ideal) distributions of control in two hypothetical companies. Tannenbaum interprets such left to right slopes as showing a hierarchical distribution in which there is a sharp reduction in control from one level to the next down the hierarchy. Companies A and B show in their actual hierarchies of control the classical view of the industrial firm. Tannenbaum finds that in practically all manufacturing organizations in Western industrialized nations, all the employees whether bosses or subordinates report the steeply graded hierarchy that he sees as divisive, and fraught with resentment and hostility.

This may be unavoidable in large-scale manufacturing, and even ideal slopes (plots of the responses to the 'should' question) do not fundamentally challenge the basic hierarchy of control. No one in manufacturing organizations suggests anything other than that upper levels should have more control than lower levels – the slope does not flatten out nor tip the other way – but the *degree* of differentiation *is* challenged. The ideal slope is often less steep. Lower level employees frequently feel that they themselves should have more say in what goes on, as in the hypothetical ideal slope for Company B which is more democratic than the actual slope.

Further, not only might the steeply graded hierarchies in large-scale industrial organizations be levelled out to some degree, but it is also possible to manage them in ways that mitigate the hierarchy's negative effects. American supervisors, for example, treat their subordinates more as equals, with relative informality, as compared to the typical authoritarian approach in Italian plants.

Tannenbaum recognizes that Italian workers may be more concerned with changing the system than with the possibility of working better. Certainly a nation's socio-economic system is embodied in forms of organization which affect hierarchy. The slope of control graphs from Yugoslav plants (which have workers' councils) and from Israeli kibbutzim (which have collective ownership and elected managers) are not as steep as those from capitalistic Western enterprises, which is not to say that the Yugoslavs and Israelis could or should be copied everywhere else, for Yugoslav managers can be authoritarian, and the kibbutz system is probably only possible in small-scale units.

The type of membership that is appropriate to the purpose of the organization also affects control. In organizations that depend on a voluntary membership (such as American trade unions and the American League of Women Voters) the rank and file exert much greater influence than do the paid employees in industry; and similar results in Brazilian development banks staffed by highly educated professionals suggest that professionalization has the same effect because these members are relied on to do their work with less direct control, and more attention is paid to their views.

However, though the slope of the line in a control graph is its most instantly obvious feature, it does not in Tannenbaum's view depict the most important feature of an organization which, he says, is the *total control* within an organization, as depicted on the graph by the *area* beneath the line. In the graph both companies have identical hierarchical slopes but the line for Company A is higher than that for Company B, so the area beneath the line for Company A (i.e. between the line and the lateral axis at the base of the graph) is greater. In other words, the influence scores for all groups are greater, so that everyone has more control. Here is the visual representation of the apparent paradox that lower level employees such as workers can have greater control and yet not detract from the control exercised by managers. Indeed, managers too may then have greater control. This is possible because the total amount of influence, the size of the 'influence pie', can be expanded – and can be greater in one organization than in another. In this sense organizations are not fixed but are 'variable states'.

Tannenbaum points out that the leaders are also the led. Superiors depend on their subordinates to get things done. If superiors assume an expandable amount of total control, they can communicate readily with subordinates, welcome opinions, and take up suggestions; in other words, invite influence over themselves. At the same time, the involvement of subordinates in what is being done means that the superior's influence expands also, for they are more likely to do what needs to be done. The authoritarian boss who assumes a fixed amount of total control and clings to what he perceives as his rightful share may look as if he is dominating everyone but his actual influence on what they do may be very little. Others also act on this assumption, so that each group defends its share and conflict and minimal cooperation prevail.

Research results do suggest that greater effectiveness of an organization, in terms of morale and productivity, is likely to be linked more to increasing the total amount of control than to democratizing its hierarchical distribution, because all concerned are more fully controlled and in control through interlocking influence. This is true as much of privately owned American firms as it is of collectively owned Israeli kibbutzim.

Tannenbaum's research challenges the commonplace view that control is and should be unilateral, from the leaders to the led. Leaders have greater control when the led also have greater control. Though diminishing the slope of hierarchies can be important, too much attention is paid to this 'power equalization' and too little to the possibilities of expanding the total. The evidence suggests that people are more interested in exercising more control themselves than in exactly how much others may have.

The strength of Tannenbaum's challenging perspective is that it is based on a uniquely sustained series of research projects in many countries, using standard methods, which have confirmed the results again and again.

Bibliography

Tannenbaum, A. S., *Social Psychology of the Work Organization,* Belmont, CA: Wadsworth, 1966.

Tannenbaum, A. S., *Control in Organizations,* McGraw-Hill, 1968.

Tannenbaum, A. S., Kavcic, B., Rosner, M., Vianello, M., and Wieser, G., *Hierarchy in Organizations,* Jossey-Bass, 1974.

Tannenbaum, A. S., and Cooke, R. A., 'Organizational Control: A Review of Studies Employing the Control Graph Method,' in C. J. Lammers and D. J. Hickson (eds.), *Organizations Alike and Unlike,* London: Routledge & Kegan Paul, 1979.

Eric Trist and the work of the Tavistock Institute

Eric Trist is a social psychologist who for over twenty years was the senior member of the Tavistock Institute of Human Relations, London. During that time he conducted, with a number of colleagues (including F. E. Emery and the late A. K. Rice), a programme of research and consultancy investigations into the structure and functioning of organizations from a 'systems' point of view. He is currently affiliated with the Wharton School of the University of Pennsylvania where he is Emeritus Professor and Chairman of the Management and Behavioral Science Research Center, and with York University, Ontario, where he is Professor of Environmental Studies.

In collaboration with K. W. Bamforth (an ex-miner) Trist studied the effects of mechanization in British coal mining. With the advent of coal-cutters and mechanical conveyors, the degree of technical complexity of coal-getting was raised to a higher level. Mechanization made possible the working of a single long face in place of a series of short faces, but this technological change had a number of social and psychological consequences for the work organization and the worker's place in it, to which little thought was given before the change was introduced. The pattern of organization in short face working was based on a small artisan group of a skilled man and his mate, assisted by one or more labourers. The basic pattern around which the work relationships in the longwall method were organized is the coal face group of forty to fifty men, their shot-firer and 'deputies' (i.e. supervisors). Thus the basic unit in mining took on the characteristics in size and structure of a small factory department, and in doing so disrupted the traditional high degree of job autonomy and close work relationships with a number of deleterious effects.

The mass production character of the longwall method necessitates a large-scale mobile layout advancing along the seam, basic task specialization according to shift, and very specific job roles with different methods of payment within each shift. In these circumstances there are considerable problems of maintaining effective communications and good working relations between forty men spatially spread over two hundred yards in a tunnel, and temporally spread over twenty-four hours in three successive shifts. From the production engineering point of view it is possible to write an equation that 200 tons equals 40 men over 200 yards over 24 hours, but the psychological and social problems raised are of a new order when the work organization transcends the limits of the traditional, small face-to-face group undertaking the complete task itself. The social integration of the previous small groups having been disrupted by the new technology, and little attempt made to achieve any new integration, many symptoms of social stress occur. Informal cliques which develop to help each other out can only occur over small parts of the face, inevitably leaving some isolated; individuals react defensively using petty deceptions with regard to timekeeping and reporting of work; they compete for allocation to the best work-places; there is mutual scapegoating across shifts, each blaming the other for inadequacies (since in the new system with its decreased autonomy, no one individual can normally be pinpointed with the blame, scapegoating of the absent shift becomes self-perpetuating and resolves nothing). Absenteeism becomes a way of the miner compensating himself for the difficulties of the job.

This study of the effects of technological change led Trist to develop the concept of the working group as being neither a technical system nor a social system, but as an interdependent socio-technical system. The technological demands place limits on the type of work organization possible, but the work organization has social and psychological properties of its own that are independent of the technology. From this point of view it makes as little sense to regard social relationships as being determined by the technology as it does to regard the manner in which a job is performed as being determined by the social–psychological characteristics of the workers. The social and technical requirements are mutually inter-active and they must also have economic validity, which is a third interdependent aspect. The attainment of optimum conditions for any one of these aspects does not necessarily result in optimum conditions for the system as a whole, since interference will occur if the others are inadequate. The aim should be joint optimization.

In further studies of mining, Trist found that it was possible, within the same technological and economic constraints, to operate different systems of work organization with different social and psychological effects, thus underlining the considerable degree of organizational choice which is available to management to enable them to take account of the social and psychological aspects. A third form of operation known as the 'composite longwall method' was developed which enabled mining to benefit from the new technology while at the same time allowing some of the characteristics of the shortwall method to be continued. In the composite system, groups of men are responsible for the whole task, allocate themselves to shifts and to jobs within the shift, and are paid on a group bonus. Thus the problems of over-specialized work roles, segregation of tasks across shifts with consequent scapegoating and lack of group cohesion were overcome. For example, it became common for a sub-group that had finished its scheduled work for a shift before time, to carry on with the next activity in the sequence in order to help those men on the subsequent shift who were members of their group. The composite longwall method was quite comparable in technological terms with the conventional longwall method, but it led to greater productivity, lower cost, considerably less absenteeism and accidents, and greater work satisfaction, since it was a socio-technical system which was better geared to the workers' social and psychological needs for job autonomy and close working relationships.

This socio-technical system approach was also applied to supervisory roles by Rice in studies of an Indian textile firm. He found that it was not enough to allocate to the supervisor a list of responsibilities (see Fayol, p. 64) and perhaps insist upon a particular style of handling men (see Likert, p. 164). The supervisor's problems arise from a need to control and coordinate a system of men–task relationships, and in particular to manage the 'boundary conditions', that is, those activities of this system which relate it to the larger system of which it is a part. In order to do this effectively, it is necessary to have an easily identifiable arrangement of tasks so that it is possible to maximize the autonomous responsibility of the group itself for its own internal control, thus freeing the supervisor for his primary task of boundary management.

In an automatic weaving shed for example, in which the occupational roles had remained unchanged since hand weaving, the activities of the shed were broken down into component tasks, with the number of workers required determined by work studies of the separate tasks. Those in different occupational tasks worked on different numbers of looms; weavers operated 24 or 32, battery fillers charged the batteries of 48, smash hands served 75, jobbers 112, the bobbin carrier 224, etc. This resulted in the shift manager having to interact about the job regularly with all the remaining 28 workers on his shift, jobbers having to interact with 14, smash hands with 9, a weaver with 7, etc., all on the basis of individual interactions aggregated together only at the level of the whole shift, with no stable internal group structure. Rice carried through a reorganization to create 4 work groups of 6 men, each with a group leader, each with an identifiable group task and a new set of interdependent work roles to carry it out. The boundaries of these groups were more easily delineated, and thus the work leader's task in their management facilitated. As a result there was a considerable and sustained improvement in efficiency and decrease in damage.

These studies and others of the Tavistock Institute have led Emery and Trist to conceptualize the enterprise as an 'open socio-technical system'. 'Open' because it is a system concerned with obtaining inputs from its environment and exporting outputs to its environment, as well as operating the conversion process in between. They regard the organization not in terms of a closed physical system which can obtain a stable resolution of forces in static equilibrium, but in the light of the modern biological concept of an open system (due to von Bertalanffy) in which the equilibrium obtained by the organism or the organization is essentially dynamic having a continual interchange across the boundaries with its environment. Indeed, they would regard the primary task of the management of the enterprise as a whole as that of relating the total system to its environment through the regulation of the boundary interchanges, rather than that of internal regulation. A management which takes its environment as given and concentrates on organizing internally in the most efficient way is pursuing a dangerous course. This does not mean that top management should not be involved in internal problems, but that such involvement must be oriented to the environmental opportunities and demands.

The problem is that environments are changing at an increasing rate and towards increasing complexity. Factors in the environment, over which the organization has no control or even no knowledge, may interact to cause significant changes. Emery and Trist have classified environments according to their degree of complexity from that of a placid, randomized environment (corresponding to the economist's perfect competition) to that of a 'turbulent field' in which significant variances arise not only from competitive organizations involved but also from the field (e.g. market) itself. They present a case history of an organization which failed to appreciate that its environment was changing from a relatively placid to a relatively turbulent one. This company in the British food canning industry had, for a long period, held 65 per cent of the market for its main product – a tinned vegetable. On this basis the company invested in a new automatic factory, and in doing so incorporated an inbuilt rigidity – the necessity for long runs. But even whilst the factory was being built, several changes in the environment were taking place over which the organization had no control. The development of frozen foods, and the increasing affluence which enabled more people to afford these, presented consumers with an alternative. Greater direct competition came from the existence of surplus crops which American frozen food manufacturers sold off very cheaply due to their inappropriateness for freezing, their use by a number of small British *fruit* canning firms with surplus capacity due to the seasonal nature of imported fruit, and the development of supermarkets and chain stores with a wish to sell more goods under their house names. As the small canners provided an extremely cheap article (having no marketing costs and a cheaper raw material) they were able within three years to capture over 50 per cent of a shrinking market. This is a clear example of the way in which factors in the environment interact directly to produce a considerable turbulence in the field of the organization's operations, which, in the case of the vegetable canning factory, required a large redefinition of the firm's purpose, market and product mix before a new dynamic equilibrium was obtained.

Emery and Trist maintain that enterprises like the food canner are designing their organization structures to be appropriate to simpler environments rather than the complex turbulent ones which they are actually facing. A new *design principle* is now required. Organizations by their very nature require what is known in systems theory and information theory as 'redundancy'. By this is meant duplication, replaceability, interchangeability, and these resources are needed to reduce error in the face of variability and change. The traditional technocratic bureaucracy is based on *redundancy of parts*. The parts are broken down so that the ultimate elements are as simple as possible; thus an unskilled worker in a narrow job who is cheap to replace and who takes little time to train would be regarded as an ideal job design. But this approach also requires reliable control systems – often cumbersome and costly.

An alternative design, based on the *redundancy of functions*, is appropriate to turbulent environments. In this approach individuals and units have wide repertoires of activities to cope with change and they are self-regulating. For the individual they create roles rather than mere jobs; for the organization, they bring into being a *variety-increasing* system rather than the traditional control by variety reduction. For this approach to be achieved there has to be continuing development of appropriate new values concerned with improving the *quality of working life* by keeping the technological determinants of worker behaviour to a minimum in order to satisfy social and psychological needs by the involvement of all involved. Autonomous working groups, collaboration rather than competition (between organizations as well as within them) and reduction of hierarchical emphasis, are some of the requirements for operating effectively in modern turbulence. The table on page 90 sets out the key features of the old and new approaches.

The socio-technical systems approach to jointly achieving effective functioning in a turbulent environment, and to increasing the quality of working life, has also been undertaken at a wider 'macro-social' level. For example, working with the Norwegian social psychologists E. Thorsrud and P. G. Herbst, the Tavistock group have studied the Norwegian shipping industry.

Many technological designs are available for sophisticated bulk carriers. The one chosen was that which best met the social and psychological needs of the small shipboard community that had to live together in isolated conditions, twenty-four hours a day for considerable periods, while efficiently achieving the work tasks. A common mess and a recreation room were established; deck and engine-room crews were integrated, status differences between officers and men were reduced and even eliminated through the

Features of Old and New Approaches

Old Approach	New Approach
The technological imperative	Joint optimization
People as extensions of machines	People as complementary to machines
People as expendable spare parts	People as a resource to be developed
Maximum task breakdown, simple narrow skills	Optimum task grouping, multiple broad skills
External controls (supervisors, specialist staffs, procedures)	Internal controls (self-regulating sub-systems)
Tall organization chart, autocratic style	Flat organization chart, participative style
Competition, gamesmanship	Collaboration, collegiality
Organization's purposes only	Members' and society's purposes also
Alienation	Commitment
Low risk-taking	Innovation

from Trist (1981)

development of open career lines and the establishment of 'all officer' ships. Also training for future jobs onshore could be begun at sea.

Without these improvements in the quality of working life not enough Norwegians would have gone to sea to sustain the Norwegian Merchant Marine, which is critical for Norway's economy. Poorly educated and transient foreign crews could not cope with technically sophisticated ships, and alcoholism was dangerously high. These issues could not have been effectively tackled by any one single company; all firms in the industry, several seafaring unions and a number of maritime regulatory organizations all had to be involved in order to sustain the macro-social system development that was required.

The work of Trist and the Tavistock group has been most consistent in applying systems thinking over a large range of sites; the primary work system, the whole organization system and the macro-social domain. In doing so they have illuminated the dynamic nature of organizations and their functioning, the crucial importance of boundary management, and the need for a new approach to organizational design which can accommodate environmental change.

Bibliography

Emery, F. E., and Trist, E. L., 'Socio-technical systems',' in C. W. Churchman and M. Verhulst (eds.), *Management Science, Models and Techniques,* vol. 2, Pergamon, 1946; reprinted in F. E. Emery (ed.), *Systems Thinking,* Vol. I, New York: Viking-Penguin, 1981.

Trist, E. L., and Bamforth, K. W., 'Some social and psychological consequences of the Longwall method of coal getting', *Human Relations* 4 (1951), 3-38; reprinted in D. S. Pugh (ed.), *Organization Theory,* 2d edn, New York: Viking-Penguin, 1984.

Trist, E. L., et al., *Organizational Choice,* London: Tavistock, 1963.

Emery, F. E., and Trist, E. L., 'The causal texture of organizational environments', *Human Relations* 18 (1965), 21-32; reprinted in F. E. Emery (ed.), *Systems Thinking,* Vol. I, New York: Viking-Penguin, 1986.

Trist, E. L., 'The Socio-technical Perspective', in A. van de Ven and W. F. Joyce (eds.), *Perspectives on Organization Design and Behaviour,* Wiley-Interscience, 1981.

Rice, A. K., *Productivity and Social Organization,* Tavistock, 1958.

Emery, F. E., and Thorsrud, E., *Democracy at Work,* Martinus Nijhoft (Leiden), 1976.

Herbst, P. G., *Alternatives to Hierarchies,* Martinus Nijhoft (Leiden), 1976.

David Silverman

David Silverman is Principal Lecturer in Sociology at Goldsmiths' College, a constituent college of the University of London, England. He went to Goldsmiths' after a period of study in the United States. He has always worked within the discipline of sociology and his interest has been to develop a sociological critique of organizational theory. Much of his research work has been carried out in public sector organizations, including the British National Health Service, and has concentrated on selection processes and administrative occupations.

Silverman's main contribution has been the introduction of an 'action-oriented' perspective to organization theory. He has argued that an alternative is needed to what he regards as the dominant perspective in the study of organizations, namely, systems theory. The alternative is to view organizations as the product of the actions and interactions of motivated people pursuing purposes of their own. For Silverman most organizational analysis has been based on a mistaken set of assumptions, the basic mistake being to conceptualize organizations as systems which can be described and understood without reference to the motivations and interpretations of the people in them. Most organizations theory involves *reification*, that is, attributing thought and action to social constructs.

Organizational analysis started as a separate area of study, Silverman maintains, by trying to offer answers to questions posed by those who control the operation of organizations, namely, the managers. This has led to a consistent bias through which the analysis of organizations is presented in a dehumanized, neutral way while in fact it is the concerns of managers that are dealt with. This bias is apparent in all established approaches and it is Silverman's purpose to expose such biases and to set up a more satisfactory theory.

By contrast, Silverman distinguishes three characteristics of a formal organization. The first is that it arises at a discernible point in time and is easier than most sets of social relationships to perceive as an artefact. The second is that relationships are taken less for granted by those organizational members who seek to coordinate and control. The third characteristic is that planned changes in social relations and the rules of the game are open to discussion. Thus this definition looks at organizations from the point of view of the social relationships within them and how organizational 'actors' (i.e. the members) interpret and understand them. Silverman's criticisms of organization theory are based on this view.

The dominant theoretical view of organizations sees them as systems and is concerned with general patterns and points of similarity between all organizations, rather than with individual action. A systems view sees organizations as a set of interdependent parts with needs for survival. In adapting to these needs organizations are seen as behaving and taking action. Organizations have to transform a variety of inputs (men, money, materials) into outputs and the process of regulation through which this occurs has been a predominant area of study. But systems theorists fail to consider that it is the *members* of organizations, interpreting what they understand as the environment, importing meanings and common definitions, who do the regulating and adapting.

Because, like so much organizational analysis, systems theory starts from the viewpoint of the executive, it confuses the actions of managers with the behaviour of the organization. In carrying out this abstraction, systems theory directs attention away from purposive human action. Such an approach sees structures as *transcendental*, that is, with a logic of their own and analysable independently of human actions, perceptions and meanings. Silverman sees structures as *immanent*, that is, continuously constructed and reconstructed out of the meanings that actors take from them and give to them. These differences in approach are at the heart of conceptualizing organizations. Given these theoretical structures, the same problems are to be found in the two main variants of systems theory: *functionalism* which is derived from sociology and *sociotechnical systems* theory which is inter-disciplinary in character. They are both concerned with the consequences rather than the causes of behaviour. They both rest on a biological analogy which is unsatisfactory for the description and explanation of human events. They both stress processes of adaptation and states of equilibrium and cannot adequately deal with change and conflict. They both involve reification rather than dealing with the sources of orientations of organizational members.

However, within these rather severe limitations, Silverman does see some limited steps forward in the socio-technical systems perspective. The idea of behaviour and motivations as an outcome of technology has involved some writers dealing with conflicts of interests and strategies. Seeing organizations as interrelations of technology, environment, sentiments and structures, with no one factor dominant, means stressing the absence of any one most efficient form of organization. But in the end any form of systems approach is unable to explain why particular organizations occur; it can only describe patterns of adaptation and their consequences in its own terms.

Silvermán also sees problems with the other main approach that he identifies, *organizational psychology*. There is not here the issue of reification and there is a concern with people. But, as with systems theory, the emphasis is still on needs; almost, people as systems. Individuals are conceptualized as having needs to fulfil (e.g. physiological, social, self-actualizing) which form a hierarchy and are often in conflict with organizational goals. Silverman suggests that there are major problems in validating the existence of such needs and that it is not clear whether they would explain behaviour anyway. Also, writers in this approach are far too concerned with general patterns of need and behaviour rather than individual action which, for Silverman, should be at the heart of organizational analysis.

To deal with all the problems inherent in established ways of theorizing about organizations there is only one solution, the adoption of an *action frame of reference*. The essential element in this approach is to view organizations as the outcome of the interaction of motivated people who are attempting to resolve their own problems and pursue their own ends. The environment is conceptualized as a source of meanings for organizational members, being made up of other actors who are defining situations in ways which allow actors inside organizations to defend their own actions and make sense of the actions of others. Some are given significance, others are not. Actions have no meaning other than those given to them by actors.

This method of analysis and theoretical approach is illustrated and developed in the work that Silverman has carried out with Jill Jones on staff-selection interviews in public sector organizations. In empirical terms the emphasis on action, social construction of reality and the development of shared orientations leads to an emphasis on the study of language. It is through language that actions, perceptions and meanings of organizational rules, for example, are established and continuously reaffirmed.

Selection is thus not an objective process of getting the right man for the job, but a case of making sense of what goes on in a socially organized setting. In an interview situation, the actors may start with conflicting views of reality or the facts. An outcome has to be managed through verbal exchanges to arrive at an acceptable 'account' of the character of the interviewee and the process of selection. In doing this the actors usually confirm the existing structures of power and authority, shared meanings and rules of operation. The selection process is important in confirming the actor's understanding of what happens and why in the particular organizations of which they are members.

What happens in organizations, then, is a continuous product of motivated human action. For Silverman this is merely emphasizing a general principle of all social life. Because of this it is difficult to distinguish organizations as entities from other types of social structures – and not worth it. The study of organizations should not be seen as an end in itself but as a setting within which general social processes can be studied from a clear *sociological* perspective. By doing this it is possible to ensure that the analyst does not impose his own or management's view of what the issues and problems are.

Bibliography

Silverman, D., *The Theory of Organizations,* London: Heinemann, 1970.
Silverman, D., and Jones, J., *Organizational Work: The Language of Grading: The Grading of Language,* Collier Macmillan, 1976.

C. Northcote Parkinson

C. Northcote Parkinson 'is an Englishman with a distinguished academic career who has been writing scholarly books since 1934'. He has taught at the Universities of Malaya, Liverpool and Illinois, and now devotes himself full-time to writing.

Parkinson confronts the manifest fact that there is little or no relationship between the work to be done in an organization and the size of staff doing it. The growth of administrative hierarchies may be independent of the work itself. To explain this phenomenon he propounds Parkinson's Law that 'work expands to fill the time available for its completion'.

As a graphic analogy with the world of administration, he cites the case of the elderly lady with nothing else to do, who spends an entire day sending a postcard to her niece, ending 'prostrate after a day of doubt, anxiety and toil'. This is because having nothing else to do she elevates each single activity such as finding a pen and a stamp, and getting to the post box, into a major effort which demands much time and energy. In the same way, an administrative task in an organization can either be regarded as incidental and done in a few minutes, or it can be elevated to a series of component tasks each of which makes demands so great that in total they fill the working day.

Small wonder, then, that administrative officials find themselves overworked. What they will do about it is foretold by the motivational axiom 'an official wants to multiply subordinates, not rivals'. Hence rather than share the work with colleague B, overworked official A appoints subordinates C and D. By appointing two, A preserves his own position of being the only official comprehending the entire range of work. When C inevitably complains of overwork, A preserves equity by allowing C to have subordinates E and F and also by allowing D to appoint G and H. With this staff, A's own promotion is now virtually certain. Moreover, by this stage a second axiom has taken effect, 'officials make work for each other'. For seven are now doing what one did before, but the routing of drafts, minutes and incoming documents between them ensures that all are working hard and that A is working harder than ever.

Parkinson cites impressive evidence of this process. The British Navy Estimates disclose that over the first half of this century while the numbers of ships and of officers and men declined, the numbers of Admiralty and dockyard officials increased rapidly. Indeed, the men of Whitehall increased nearly 80 per cent, and it may be concluded that this would have occurred had there been no seamen at all. Similarly in the Colonial Office. In 1947 and again in 1954 the figures for staff had risen substantially even though during and after the war the size of the Empire had markedly shrunk.

Once constituted, administrative hierarchies are bestrewn with committees, councils and boards, through which the weightier matters of finance must pass. Now since a million is real only to a millionaire, these committees and the like are necessarily made up of persons accustomed to think in tens or hundreds, perhaps in thousands, but never more than this. The result is a typical pattern of committee work which may be stated as the Law of Triviality. It means 'that the time spent on any item of the agenda will be in inverse proportion to the sum involved'.

Thus a contract for a £10,000,000 atomic reactor will be passed with a murmur of agreement, after formal reference to the engineers' and the geophysicists' reports and to plans in appendices. In such cases the Law of Triviality is supplemented by technical factors, since half the committee including the chairman do not know what a reactor is and half the rest do not know what it is for. Rather than face these difficulties of explanation, any member who does know will decide it is better to say nothing despite his misgivings about the whole thing. However, when the agenda reaches the question of a roof for the bicycle shed, here is both a topic and a sum of money which everyone understands. Now all can show they are pulling their weight and make up for their silence over the reactor. Discussion will go on for at least forty-five minutes, and a saving of some £100 may be satisfactorily achieved.

Of course, such a committee will have passed the size of approximately 21 members, which Parkinson's Coefficient of Inefficiency (a formula is given) predicts as critical. Where such a number is reached, conversations occur at both ends of the table, and to be heard a member has to rise. Once on his feet, he cannot help making a speech, if only from force of habit. At this point the efficient working of a committee becomes impossible.

This might have happened in any case from self-induced 'injelitis' – the disease of induced inferiority. From an examination of moribund institutions it has been ascertained that the source infection comes from the arrival in an organization's hierarchy of an individual combining both incompetence and jealousy. At a certain concentration these qualities react to induce 'injelitance'; soon the head of the organization, who is second-rate, sees to it that his subordinates are all third-rate, and they see to it that their subordinates are fourth-rate, and so on. The organization accepts its mediocrity and ceases to attempt to match better organizations. After all, since little is done mistakes are rare, and since aims are low, success is complete.

The characteristics of organizations can be assessed even more easily than this, simply by their physical accoutrements. Publishers, for example, or again research establishments, frequently flourish in shabby and makeshift quarters. Lively and productive as these may be, who is not impressed by the contrasting institution with an imposing and symmetrical façade, within which shining floors glide to a receptionist murmuring with carmine lips into an ice-blue receiver.

However, it is now known that a perfection of planned layout is achieved only by institutions on the point of collapse. During exciting discovery or progress there is no time to plan the perfect headquarters. This comes afterwards – and too late. Thus by the time the Palace of Nations at Geneva was opened in 1937, the League had practically ceased to exist. The British Empire expanded whilst the Colonial Office was in haphazard accommodation, and contracted after it moved into purpose-built accommodation in 1875. The conduct of the Second World War was planned in crowded and untidy premises in Washington, the elaborate layout of the Pentagon at Arlington, Virginia, being constructed later.

In public affairs there is a propensity for expenditure on elaborate and inappropriate constructions such as those mentioned, as indeed for any other kind of expenditure. In fact, all forms of administration are prone to expenditure. This is due to the effects of Parkinson's Second Law that 'expenditure rises to meet income'. The widely understood domestic phenomenon which unfailingly appears after each increase in the husband's income is equally prevalent in administration: with the important difference in government administration that expenditure rises towards a ceiling that is not there. Were revenue to be reduced there would actually be an improvement in services. The paradox of administration is that if there were fewer officials each would have *less* to do and therefore more time to think about what he was doing.

Turning more recently to the business corporation, Parkinson's historical eye provides a lively view of tycoons and their giant creations. His whimsical and colourful résumés of how the world's biggest businesses came to be what they are do not overlook their degrading and polluting consequences. At the same time, Parkinson's serious conclusion from his stories of the multi-national corporations and their most famous or infamous bosses is that their control requires a more international form of government, not a futile attempt to return to nationalistic control. Thus the growth of the multi-nationals could unintentionally lead to a global political gain, for: 'Set quite apart from the blood-stained arena of nationalism is the new world of big business, a world where the jealousies of the nation states are actually forgotten'.

Bibliography

Parkinson, C. N., *Parkinson's Law and Other Studies in Administration,* Murray, 1958, Penguin, 1965, Ballantine, 1975.

Parkinson, C. N., *The Law and the Profits,* Murray, 1960, Penguin, 1965.

Parkinson, C. N., *Big Business,* Little, Brown, 1974.

Parkinson, C. N., *The Rise of Big Business,* Weidenfeld & Nicolson, 1977.

3 · *Decision-making in Organizations*

The task of administration is so to design this environment that the individual will approach as close as practicable to rationality (judged in terms of the organization's goals) in his decisions.

Herbert A. Simon

Interesting people and interesting organizations ... need to supplement the technology of reason with a technology of foolishness.

James G. March

An administrator often feels more confident when 'flying by the seat of his pants' than when following the advice of theorists.

Charles E. Lindblom

It makes more sense to talk about participative and autocratic situations than it does to talk about participative and autocratic managers.

Victor H. Vroom

An organization can be considered as a set of games between groups of partners who have to play with each other.

Michel Crozier

Although many writers have considered various aspects of organizational functioning, there has been a continuing school of thought which maintains that it is the analysis of decision-making which is *the* key to understanding organizational management processes.

This approach was inaugurated by Herbert A. Simon and his colleagues of Carnegie-Mellon University. For Simon, management *is* decision-making and his colleagues Richard Cyert and James March have developed this approach to consider a behavioural theory of the firm, Charles Lindblom looks at decision-making in relation to public policy and discovers a 'science of muddling-through'.

Victor Vroom proposes a theory of appropriate decision-making styles and Michel Crozier examines the nature of the power which is at the basis of the decision-making 'game'.

Herbert A. Simon

Herbert Simon is a distinguished American political and social scientist whose perceptive contributions have influenced thinking and practice in many fields. He began his career in public administration and operations research, but as he took appointments in successive universities his interests encompassed all aspects of administration. He is Professor of Computer Science and Psychology at Carnegie-Mellon University, Pittsburgh, where he and his colleagues have been engaged on fundamental research into the processes of decision-making, using computers to simulate human thinking. Herbert Simon's outstanding intellectual contribution was publicly recognized when, in 1978, he was awarded the Nobel Prize for Economics.

For Simon 'management' is equivalent to 'decision-making' and his major interest has been an analysis of how decisions are made and of how they might be made more effectively.

He describes three stages in the overall process of making a decision:

1. Finding occasions calling for a decision – the *intelligence* activity (using the word in the military sense).
2. Inventing, developing and analysing possible courses of action – the *design* activity.
3. Selecting a particular course of action from those available – the *choice* activity.

Generally speaking, intelligence activity precedes design, and design activity precedes choice; but the sequence of stages can be much more complex than this. Each stage in itself can be a complex decision-making process. The design stage can call for new intelligence activities. Problems at any stage can generate a series of sub-problems which in turn have their intelligence, design and choice stages. Nevertheless, in the process of organizational decision-making these three general stages can be discerned.

Carrying out the decisions is also regarded as a decision-making process. Thus after a policy decision has been taken, the executive having to carry it out is faced with a wholly new set of problems involving decision-making. Executing policy amounts to making more detailed policy. Essentially, for Simon, all managerial action is decision-making.

On what basis does the administrator make his decisions? The traditional theory of the economists assumed complete rationality. The 'model' was that of an 'economic man' who deals with the 'real world' in all its complexity, and who selects the rationally determined best course from among all those available to him in order to maximize his returns. But clearly this model is divorced from reality. We know that there is a large non-rational, emotional and unconscious element in man's thinking and behaviour. The need for an administrative theory is precisely because there are practical limits to human rationality. These limits to rationality are not static but depend upon the organizational environment in which the individual's decision takes place. It then becomes the task of administration, says Simon, 'so to design this environment that the individual will approach as close as practicable to rationality (judged in terms of the organization's goals) in his decisions'.

In place of 'economic man' Simon proposes a model of 'administrative man'. While economic man maximizes (i.e. selects the best course from those available to him), administrative man 'satisfices' – he looks for a course of action that is satisfactory or 'good enough'. In this process he is content with gross simplifications, taking into account only those comparatively few relevant factors which his mind can manage to encompass. 'Most human decision-making, whether individual or organizational, is concerned with the discovery and selection of satisfactory alternatives; only in exceptional cases is it concerned with the discovery and selection of optimal alternatives.' Most decisions are concerned not with searching for the sharpest needle in the haystack but with searching for a needle sharp enough to sew with. Thus administrative man can make decisions without searching for all the possible alternatives and can use relatively simple rules of thumb. In business terms he does not look for 'maximum profit' but 'adequate profit'; not 'optimum price' but 'fair price'. This makes his world much simpler.

What techniques of decision-making are then available? In discussing this problem, Simon makes a distinction between two polar types of decisions: *programmed* and *non-programmed* decisions. These are not mutually exclusive but rather make up a continuum stretching from highly programmed decisions at one end to highly unprogrammed decisions at the other. Decisions are programmed to the extent that they are repetitive and routine or a definite procedure has been worked out to deal with them. They thus do not have to be considered afresh each time they occur. Examples would be the decisions involved in processing a customer's order, determining an employee's sickness benefit or carrying out any routine job.

Decisions are unprogrammed to the extent that they are new and unstructured or where there is no cut-and-dried method for handling the problem. This may be either because it has not occurred before, or because it is particularly difficult or important. Examples would be decisions to introduce a new product, make substantial staff redundancies or move to a new location. All these decisions would be non-programmed (although entailing many programmed sub-decisions) because the organization would have no detailed strategy to govern its responses to these situations, and it would have to fall back on whatever general capacity it had for intelligent problem-solving.

Human beings are capable of acting intelligently in many new or difficult situations but they are likely to be less efficient. The cost to the organization of relying on non-programmed decisions in areas where special-purpose procedures and programmes can be developed is likely to be high and an organization should try to programme as many of its decisions as possible. The traditional techniques of programmed decision-making are habit, including knowledge and skills, clerical routines and standard operating procedures, and the organization's structure and culture, i.e. its system of common expectations, well-defined information channels, established sub-goals, etc. The traditional techniques for dealing with non-programmed decisions rely on the selection and training of executives who possess judgement, intuition and creativity. These categories of technique have been developed over thousands of years (the building of the pyramids must have involved the use of many of them). But within the last decade, Simon argues, a complete revolution in techniques of decision-making has got under way, comparable to the invention of powered machinery in manufacture.

This revolution has been due to the application of such techniques as mathematical analysis, operational research, electronic data processing and computer simulation. These were used first for completely programmed operations (e.g. mathematical calculations, accounting procedures) formerly regarded as the province of clerks. But more and more elements of judgement (previously unprogrammed and the province of middle management) can now be incorporated into programmed procedures. Decisions on stock control and production control have been in the forefront of this development. With advances in computer technology, more and more complex decisions will become programmed. Even a completely unprogrammed decision, made once and for all, can be reached via computer techniques by building a model of the decision situation. Various courses of action can then be simulated and their effects assessed. 'The automated factory of the future', Simon maintains, 'will operate on the basis of programmed decisions produced in the automated office beside it.'

Bibliography

Simon, H. A., *Administrative Behaviour,* 2nd edn, Macmillan, 1960.
Simon, H. A., *The New Science of Management Decision,* Harper & Row, 1960.
Simon, H. A., *The Shape of Automation,* Harper & Row, 1965.
March, J. G., and Simon, H. A., *Organizations,* Wiley, 1958.

Richard M. Cyert and James G. March

Richard Cyert and James March between them epitomize the development of the school of decision-making theory at what is now Carnegie-Mellon University. March's interest in processes of decision is also reflected in the distinctive sophistication of his many publications on the nature of power. Cyert continued at Carnegie-Mellon University and has become its President, but March moved to California where he is now Professor of Management at Stanford University, and a Senior Fellow at the Hoover Institution.

Their 'behavioural theory of the firm' is a notable effort to link classical economics theory to contemporary organization theory. It is an attempt to describe and to explain how business decisions come to be made. Cyert and March take business firms as their starting point, and specifically have in mind the large multi-product organization operating under 'imperfect competition', that is in a market where supply of and demand for the product do not move freely but can be manipulated by the firms in limited competition. The theory is about decisions such as what price to aim at, what volume to produce, and how resources are to be allocated within a firm. Decisions of these kinds are seen as choices, made in terms of objectives, from among a set of alternatives on the basis of whatever information is available.

Classical theory tends to view a firm as an entrepreneur rather than as an organization and, assuming perfect knowledge of all market conditions, stresses profit maximization as the goal. It takes a firm to be an 'omnisciently rational' system of business.

Cyert and March view a firm as an 'adaptively rational' system, adapting and responding to a variety of internal and external constraints in arriving at decisions.

Far from showing the characteristics of a single-minded entrepreneur, a business organization is composed of a number of departments with diverse interests. Decisions have to allow for these interests. But what guidelines or rules then set limits to decisions? Far from having perfect knowledge, organizations appear to act on very small portions of the total available information. If this is so, then the means by which these small selections of information come to be screened out are critical. How are they affected by internal conflicts or by pressure of time? So a business firm is constrained by its problems of internal management coordination, by the uncertainty of its external situation or environment, and by its own limited capacity for assembling, storing and utilizing information.

What does a firm look like as an information-processing and decision-making system? To begin with, it is not tidily monolithic. It is more like a shifting multiple-goal coalition. In a business organization the coalition includes managers, workers, stockholders, suppliers, customers, lawyers, tax collectors, regulatory agencies, etc., all of whom have some interest in the organization but whose goals or preferences about what should be done potentially differ. More than this, the organization splits the decisions in which coalition members are interested into subproblems and assigns the sub-problems to sub-units in the organization. In a departmental structure, the sales department handles marketing problems, the accounting department handles finance problems, and so on. Each sub-unit sees its own objectives as paramount for the goals of the firm as a whole.

Thus just as a manager needs to predict and attempt to manipulate the unstable external environment of his firm, he must predict and attempt to manipulate its internal complexities. Cyert and March have the impression that most managers devote much more time and energy to the problems of managing the 'coalition' than they do to the problems of dealing with the outside world. Decisions cannot be taken without an intricate reckoning of the interests involved and the demands of all who are interested. One result is a 'fire department' organization in which decisions are actually taken as things happen on the basis of immediate expediency, and not on the basis of far-sighted cool calculation as is supposed. For example, sales may be forecast and long-term production plans carefully developed, but actual production decisions are more often affected by the day-to-day impact of salesmen's reports, recent sales figures and inventory levels. Yet this is not as irrational as it may seem. Given that a firm is indeed a multiple-goal coalition of interests, then the firm may have learned that this pattern of behaviour best permits continual adjustment to the shifting demands of those interests.

The decision process concerns three basic characteristics of organizations, organizational goals, organizational expectations and organizational choice. That is, what shall the objectives be, what is expected to happen and what consequences are anticipated from actions which could be taken, and what action shall be chosen.

There are four features of the decision-making process, which as relational concepts taken together form a theory to explain how these decisions are arrived at. They are:

1. Quasi-resolution of conflict.
2. Uncertainty avoidance.
3. Problemistic search.
4. Organizational learning.

Quasi-resolution of conflict describes the internal condition of most organizations most of the time. Even if there is consensus of vague overall goals, when it comes to the statement of objectives to be acted upon there is no consensus. An organization is a coalition of conflicting interests. Nor do the devices for 'quasi-resolution' of these conflicts actually arrive at consensus; what they do is to enable organizations to thrive despite unresolved divergencies. The first such device is 'local rationality'. As each sub-unit or department deals with only one set of decision problems it solves these 'rationally' within its own narrow specialist perspective whether or not the total outcome for the organization over the range of sub-units is rational. Sales departments handle sales decisions and production departments production ones, and so a complex set of inter-related problems is reduced to separate simple ones even though the decisions then taken on each may be mutually inconsistent.

The second device for quasi-resolution of conflict eases this difficulty. It is 'acceptable level decision rules'. Overall optimization by the firm might require each decision to be consistent with all the others; but in fact the acceptable level of consistency is low enough to permit an outcome which is simply acceptable to all interests, rather than optimal to anything overall. Thirdly, 'sequential attention to goals' also helps to quasi-resolve conflict. Rather than commit itself to one goal or another, an organization attends first to one goal and then to another in sequence, e.g. its resolves pressures for 'smooth production' versus 'satisfy customers' (with individual design modifications) by doing first one and then the other.

Uncertainty is something with which all organizations must live. There are market uncertainties, uncertainties over supplies, uncertainties over the behaviour of shareholders and governments, and so on. But the decision processes in organizations act to avoid uncertainty. They avoid having to act on long-term forecasts by actually reacting to information here and now, and solve pressing problems rather than develop long-run strategies. They avoid having to anticipate external events by arranging a 'negotiated environment' – long contracts with suppliers and customers, adherence to industry-wide pricing conventions, and support of stable 'good business practice'.

Classical theories of choice in economics focused on the problem of choice among limited alternatives, but ignored the importance of the process of search by which the alternatives were found. *Problemistic search* is the means used by organizations to determine what choices are thought to be available. Regular planned search such as routine accumulation of market information is relatively unimportant. Search is 'motivated', i.e the occurrence of a problem spurs search for ways to handle or solve it, and once a way is found (which includes revising objectives to fit available action) then search stops. So pet projects (e.g. costs to be cut in someone else's department) look for crises to fit them (e.g. a fall in profits).

Secondly, search is 'simple-minded'. When a problem arises, search for a new solution is concentrated near the old solution. A problem is assumed to concern a particular department within whose field it apparently falls, and this department then examines possibilities not too different from whatever it is that has failed, using the limited information available to it from previously established recording and filing procedures and using personnel trained in existing standard 'good practice'. If no answer appears, search turns to vulnerable areas (e.g. research) that cannot easily demonstrate their necessity by concrete results. Thirdly, therefore, search bias inhibits radically new alternatives.

Finally, *organizational learning* takes place in the decision-making process. That is, adaptation occurs through the individual members of the organization. Adaptation of goals is brought about by assessing relevant past experience of the organization and of other comparable organizations. Changing goals bring adaptation in attention, different sets of events or problems being considered. In particular, sub-units pay most attention to those criteria of good performance on which they are usually shown to be performing well. Similarly, continual failure to find acceptable solutions eventually brings adaptation of search rules.

In summary, organizational goals change in response to the sub-goals or interests of those who form the coalition, to a minimal level of what will be accepted all round, after restricted examination of a limited selective range of information. In this way, the full complexity of decision-making is reduced to what is practicable, and uncertainty is absorbed. Organizational expectations of what may happen are likewise confined to a number of possibilities few enough and familiar enough to be practicable; and organizational choices are made from among the resulting limited alternatives. For example, budget allocations to projects or to sub-units are the outcome of a bargaining-type interaction between the interests of coalition members, rather than of abstract problem-solving calculation. The main difference between project allocation and sub-unit allocation is that sub-units last longer than projects, so historical precedents are of greater importance.

The book in which Cyert and March draw their thinking together is called *A Behavioral Theory of the Firm*, but the ideas it contains have long been applied to all kinds of organizations and not only to business firms. March and a number of colleagues have gone on to add to these ideas in the course of studies of decision-making mainly in universities and colleges in the United States, Denmark and Norway. Their vivid perspective pictures organizations as *garbage cans of choices* in which decision-making processes are *uncoupled* from the decisions made, and decision-makers might be advised to try a *technology of foolishness*. The 'world of the absurd' offers an understanding of such 'organized anarchies' which 'do not know what they are doing'.

As examples in organizations, it can be observed that individuals fight for the right to participate in decision-making, and then do not exercise that right with any vigour; that information is ignored, more is requested, and then that too is ignored; that struggles take place over the adoption of a policy, but once it is adopted there is little interest in whether or not it is implemented.

One reason for such apparent absurdities is that the process of making a decision is important for its own sake to participants or potential participants. Indeed, the process of making a decision may be more concerned with relationships among participants than with the actual decision. It is an occasion for fulfilling prior commitments, for challenging or reaffirming friendships or power positions, for acquiring status, for re-defining what is going on, for enjoying the process itself.

Given such an occasion for choice, participants work out what they are doing while they are doing it, and become aware of their goals while they are pursuing them. They do not necessarily come with their aims and ideas all ready, but find them amidst the many ambiguities engendered by the disconnected contributions of the participants. Hence, 'one can view a choice opportunity as a garbage can into which various kinds of problems and solutions are dumped by participants as they are generated'. From this point of view, 'an organization is a collection of choices looking for problems, issues and feelings looking for decision situations in which they might be aired, solutions looking for issues to which they might be the answer, and decision-makers looking for work'. So although decision-making is ordinarily thought of as an attempt to solve problems, that is often not what happens. Problems and choices are partially uncoupled. Problems are not 'solved' in that sense, rather choices are attached to a problem when they happen to make action possible, but neither the problem nor the choices may be those originally thought to have been under consideration. The outcomes of decision processes may not be intended by those involved.

Decision-making is like this because what an organization is doing is not understood by its members, and because their participation in decision-making is fluid. This fluidity comes because time is scarce. No one has time to attend to all that is happening nor to be everywhere at once, so each participant attends to some decisions only and to some parts only of any one decision process. Giving attention to one decision means that others cannot be attended to. 'Every entrance is an exit somewhere else ...' Thus to a participant timing is crucial – timing, that is, the introduction of problems and choices, and timing participation.

Participants are faced with four relatively independent streams of 'garbage' coming in. There are streams of problems, of solutions, of participants, and of choice opportunities (i.e. of occasions when decisions are expected). Faced with these, the conventional insistence on rationality is not enough. Conventional efforts to clarify aims and to maintain consistency of purpose can prevent new purposes being found. So the 'technology of reason' should be supplemented with 'a technology of foolishness'. People and organizations should sometimes act *before* they think, to give themselves a chance of finding new goals in the course of that action which they would not have foreseen had they stopped to think. This means, says March, that in decision-making we sometimes need *playfulness*. Playfulness is a deliberate (but temporary) relaxation of our normal rules so that we can experiment. We need to play with 'foolish' alternatives and *in*consistent possibilities. We need to treat goals as hypotheses to be changed, intuitions as real, hypocrisy as a transitional inconsistency, memory as an enemy of the new, and experience not as fixed history but as a theory of what happened which can be replaced by a different theory. We should be foolishly playful inside our garbage cans.

Bibliography

Cyert, R. M., and March, J. G., *A Behavioural Theory of the Firm,* Prentice-Hall, 1963.

Cohen, M. D., March, J. G., and Olsen, J. P., 'A Garbage Can Model of Organizational Choice,' *Administrative Science Quarterly* 17 (1972), 1-25.

March, J. G., and Olsen, J. P., *Ambiguity and Choice in Organizations,* Universitetsforlaget (Bergen, Norway), 1976.

Charles E. Lindblom

Charles Lindblom has long been Professor of Economics and Political Science at Yale University, and is a former director of the Yale Institution for Social and Policy Studies. He has served in a wide variety of academic and political posts including those of Guggenheim Fellow and economic adviser to the US Aid Mission to India.

Lindblom asks how decisions should be made, and how they *are* made. His description and explanation of how they are made is framed primarily in terms of public administration and political systems, but it penetrates all forms of organizations. How do administrators and managers, indeed all who have to face substantial decisions, go about it? By root or by branch?

Lindblom supposes an instance of public policy. An administrator has to formulate policy with respect to inflation (this could as easily be a marketing director formulating his firm's pricing policy). To go to the root of the matter, he should attempt to list all possible values however many there might be, such as full employment, reasonable business profits, protection of savings, stable exchange rates, and so on. He should attempt to calculate how much of each is worth how much of each of the others. This done, he can try to calculate the alternative outcomes of the virtually infinitely large number of combinations that are possible. To do so he would have to gather prodigious amounts of information, and reconsider fundamentals of theory from total central planning on the one hand to completely free market on the other. His information and his alternatives, if ever they could be fully amassed, would be beyond comprehension.

Or instead the administrator could content himself with the comparatively simple goal of a period of stable prices. He would disregard most social values and attend to only what most directly and immediately might be affected by the level of prices. He would compare primarily a limited range of alternatives already familiar to him from previous occasions, avoiding recourse to theory and fundamental alternatives. He would make a decision that could achieve some partial success for a time.

The first way by which the administrator might try to make a policy decision aspires to the *rational deductive ideal*. This requires that all values be ascertained and be stated precisely enough for them to be arranged in order of priority, that principles then be derived which would indicate what information is necessary for every possible policy alternative to be compared with every other, that full information on each be obtained, and that logical calculative deduction then lead to the best alternative. This is an ideal of science, the complete deductive system, transferred to the field of values and application. On the face of it, it corresponds to good-sense notions of care and comprehensiveness. Its contemporary techniques are operations research, systems analysis, PPB (Planning-Programming-Budgeting) and the like. If followed, it would produce a *synoptic approach* to decision-making.

Yet it is difficult to find examples of this synoptic approach. Its advocates cannot point to where it is done. It is more an ideal than something actually accomplished; for it fails to adapt to what are in reality the troublesome characteristics of decisions, decision-makers, and decision-making.

Decision-makers need a way of deciding that takes account of these characteristics. They face situations in which the sheer multiplicity of values, and differences in formulating them, prevent their being exhaustively listed. Indeed, if any such attempt at listing were made, values and priorities would be changing whilst it was being done. It would be endless. In any case, because of the different partisan interests in any decision, decision-making has to proceed by 'mutual partisan adjustment', and so has to accommodate (but not necessarily reconcile) the many values of differing interests and cannot rank one above the other in explicit priority.

Decision-makers also need a way of deciding that is adapted to their own limited problem-solving capacities (see Simon p. 104). Mentally they could not cope with the deluge of information and alternatives implied in the synoptic approach. As Lindblom puts it, 'the mind flees from comprehensiveness'. In practice, their mental capacities are unlikely to be so stretched, for usually information is incomplete and inadequate, if only because the cost of finding out everything there is to know would be insupportable. Further, the presumption that what there is to know is finite and can be found out also presumes that facts and values occupy separate compartments, whereas in actuality they do not for they are inseparable. Different facts draw attention to different values, and values reinterpret facts. Likewise, the systems of variables with which decision-makers have to contend cannot be closed off to allow the finite analysis demanded by the synoptic approach, for there are always further interactions in fluid and open systems. Problems arise and extend in many forms.

So the strategy for making decisions that is commonly used by analysts and decision-makers is not synoptic. Lindblom terms what they do the *strategy of disjointed incrementalism*, a way of proceeding by *successive limited comparisons* that is far removed from the synoptic approach required by the rational deductive ideal.

Although disjointed incrementalism cannot be the only set of adaptations used to deal with the practical difficulties of decision-making, Lindblom suggests that it is the most prevalent. It makes changes in small increments by disjointed or uncoordinated processes (an increment is 'a small change in an important variable', but there is no sharp line between the incremental and the non-incremental which is a matter of degree along a continuum). It makes an indefinite, and apparently disorderly, series of small moves away from the ills of the day rather than towards defined goals. It leaves many aspects of problems seemingly unattended.

In summary, disjointed incrementalism is *incremental, restricted, means-oriented, reconstructive, serial, remedial* and *fragmented*.

Instead of rationally rooting out all the possibilities, the analyst or decision-maker simplifies his problem by contemplating only the margins by which circumstances might – if altered – differ. He contemplates marginal and therefore comprehendable change. It follows that only a restricted number of alternatives are considered. Furthermore, the task is made manageable by considering only a restricted number of consequences for each alternative. The more remote or imponderable possibilities are left aside even if they are important, for to include them might prevent any decision being made at all.

While the conventional view is that means are adjusted to ends, the comparatively means-oriented strategy of disjointed incrementalism accepts the reverse. Ends are adjusted to means. This works both ways in a reciprocal relationship. Thus if the cost of the means of attaining the objective increases, either other means can be found, or the end objective can be changed so that it is brought within the means. Objectives can be fitted to policies as much as policies to objectives. This merges into the strategy's fourth feature, its active reconstructive response. Information is revised and reinterpreted, proposals are redesigned, and values are modified, continually. As problems are examined they are transformed.

The strategy's serial procedure is evident in its long chains of policy steps. There are never ending series of attacks on more or less permanent (though perhaps slowly changing) problems. These problems are rarely 'solved', only alleviated. The decision-maker does not look for some elusive 'solution', he looks instead for appropriate moves in a series that he expects to continue. The strategy therefore has a remedial orientation that identifies situations or ills from which to move *away*, rather than goals to move *towards*. Improvements here and there are preferred to grand aims.

Finally, disjointed incrementalism is fragmented by the way analysis and evaluation go ahead at different times, or at the same time, in many places. In the political sphere, a government policy may be under study at various times in several government departments and agencies, in universities, and in private firms and institutions (just as the policy of a single firm, for example, may be looked at by several of its departments, by its major customer, and by its bankers). Whereas the synoptic approach would try to rationally coordinate these efforts, disjointed incrementalism accepts their lack of coherence in return for the advantage of diversity. One may find what another misses. An overly controlled approach could 'coordinate out of sight' a potentially useful variety of contributions.

In these several ways the strategy of disjointed incrementalism scales problems down to size. It limits information, restricts choices, and shortens horizons so that something can be done. What is overlooked now can be dealt with later. The strategy recognizes diverse values, but discourages intransigence by those involved because its reconstructive nature avoids rules or principles which, if defined, provoke firm stands by different parties.

The result is what Lindblom has called the *science of muddling through* – a practical and sophisticated adaptation to the impossibility of attaining the synoptic ideal. As he says, an administrator often feels more confident when 'flying by the seat of his pants' than when trying to follow the advice of theorists. Disjointed incrementalism is a working strategy and not merely a failure of synoptic method. It has the virtues of its own defects, which carry it pragmatically through.

On the face of it, the strategy looks conservative. It attempts small changes which do not have far-reaching consequences. Yet radical changes may be needed. However, Lindblom points out that it is logically possible to make changes as quickly by small frequent steps as it might be by more drastic and therefore less frequent steps. Each incremental step may be relatively easy, because it is not fraught with major consequences, and at least it is a step that can be taken, whereas the enormity of a fully synoptic consideration can deter decision-makers from even making a beginning, so that it achieves no movement at all.

Bibliography

Lindblom, C. E., 'The Science of Muddling Through', *Public Administration Review* 19 (1959), 79-88.

Lindblom, C. E., *The Policy-Making Process,* Prentice-Hall, 1968.

Lindblom, C. E., and Braybrooke, D., *A Strategy of Decision,* Free Press, 1963.

Lindblom, C. E., and Cohen, D. K., *Usable Knowledge: Social Science and Social Problem Solving,* Yale University Press, 1979.

Victor H. Vroom

Victor Vroom has been involved for many years in research, teaching and consulting on the psychological analysis of behaviour in organizations. A Canadian by birth, he has been at McGill University, a number of US universities and is currently Professor and Chairman of Administrative Sciences at Yale University. His interests in the effects of personality on participation in decision-making began early and his doctoral dissertation on this topic won him the Ford Foundation Doctoral Dissertation Competition in 1959. He has also won the McKinsey Foundation Research Design Competition and the J. M. Cattell award of the American Psychological Association.

Vroom's dissertation corroborated previous findings that participation in decision-making has positive effects on attitudes and motivation. But in addition it showed that the size of these effects was a function of certain personality characteristics of the participants. Authoritarians and persons with weak independence needs are unaffected by the opportunity to participate; whereas equalitarians and those with strong independence needs develop more positive attitudes and greater motivation for effective performance through participation. The study did point out though that there are a number of different processes related to participation which might be affected differently.

Much more recently Vroom (in collaboration with P. W. Yetton and A. G. Jago) has explored in much greater depth the processes of management decision-making and the variations in subordinate participation which can come about. Possible decision processes which a manager might use in dealing with an issue affecting his group of subordinates are as follows (though there are some variations if the issue concerns one subordinate only):

AI   You solve the problem or make the decision yourself, using information available to you at that time.

AII   You obtain the necessary information from your subordinate(s), then decide on the solution to the problem yourself. You may or may not tell your subordinates what the problem is in getting the information from them. The role played by your subordinates in making the decision is clearly one of providing necessary information to you, rather than generating or evaluating alternative solutions.

CI   You share the problem with relevant subordinates individually, getting their ideas and suggestions without bringing them together as a group. Then *you* make the decisions that may or may not reflect your subordinates' influence.

CII   You share the problem with your subordinates as a group, collectively obtaining their ideas and suggestions. Then *you* make the decision that may or may not reflect your subordinates' influence.

GII   You share a problem with your subordinates as a group. Together you generate and evaluate alternatives and attempt to reach agreement (consensus) on a solution. Your role is much like that of chairman. You do not try to influence the group to adopt 'your' solution and you are willing to accept and implement any solution that has the support of the entire group.

Processes AI and AII are designated autocratic processes, CI and CII consultative processes, and GII is a group process. (GI applies to single subordinate issues.) Having identified these processes Vroom and Yetton's research programme then proceeded to answer two basic questions:

1. What decision-making processes *should* managers use to deal effectively with the problems they encounter in their jobs? This is a normative or prescriptive question. To answer it would require setting up a logical 'model' with a series of steps or procedures by which a manager could rationally determine which was the most effective process to inaugurate.

2. What decision-making processes *do* managers use in dealing with their problems and what factors affect their choice of processes and degree of subordinate participation? This is a descriptive question, and the answer is important in delineating how far away from a rational approach managers are in their decision-making. We could then ask what activities of training or development could lead managers to a more effective decision-making style.

It is in their answer to the first question that Vroom and his collaborators have made a most distinctive contribution. They have developed a detailed normative model of decision-making processes based on rational principles consistent with existing evidence on the consequences of participation for organizational effectiveness. They begin by distinguishing three classes of consequences which influence decision effectiveness:

1. The quality or rationality of the decision – clearly a process which jeopardized this would be ineffective.
2. The acceptance or commitment on the part of the subordinates to execute the decision effectively – if this commitment is necessary then processes which do not generate it even though they give a high quality decision would be ineffective.
3. The amount of time required to make the decision – a decision process which took less time, if it were equally effective, would normally be preferable to one which took longer.

These consequences generate a set of rules for the model which may then be applied to the characteristics of a manager's problem under consideration. The model will then indicate which of the decision processes is appropriate to the particular case. The model can be expressed in the form of a decision tree as shown on page 122.

In the Decision Model, the problem characteristics are presented as questions. The manager starts at the left-hand side and moves to the right along the path determined by his answer to the question above each box. At the final point of his line the model shows him which of Vroom and Yetton's decision processes he should use to reach, in the least time, a decision which will be one of quality as well as one which will be found acceptable.

As will be seen from the Decision Model, all decision processes (autocratic, consultative, group) are applicable in some circumstances and how often each should be used will depend on the type of decisions that the manager has to take. The normative model requires that all managers, if they are to be rational and effective, have to be able to operate across the whole range.

The research undertaken by Vroom and Yetton to answer their second question – how do managers actually behave? – is based on

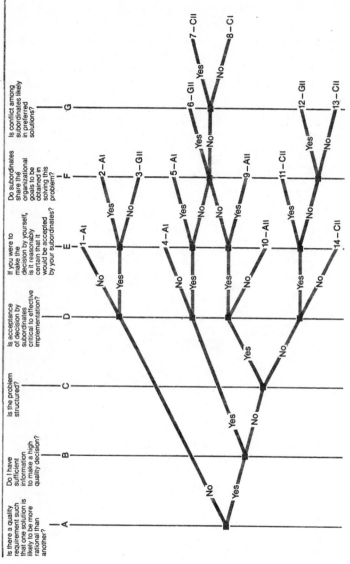

Decision Model (from Vroom and Yetton, 1973).

two methods. In the first, many managers were asked to recall decision problems and how they tackled them in terms of the questions of the Decision Model. The second method involved many managers assessing a set of standardized problem descriptions and giving their preferred solutions.

The most striking finding of these descriptive studies was that, while there were certainly average differences between managers in their use of various decision processes, these were small in comparison with the *range* of processes used by any individual manager. No manager indicated that he would use the same process on all decisions and most used all five of the decision processes above under some circumstances. 'It makes more sense to talk about participative and autocratic situations than it does to talk about participative and autocratic managers.'

The descriptive research also enabled a comparison of what managers do (or say they would do) and what the model would designate as rational behaviour. On average, a 'typical' manager was found to use the same decision process as that required by the Decision Model in 40 per cent of the situations. In a further quarter of the situations he used a process which is called 'feasible' in that it satisfied the constraints of the model on protecting decision quality and acceptability but it would not be the least time-consuming. Only in about one third of the situations did the typical manager initiate a process which will risk quality or acceptability. In addition it was found that the constraints necessary to achieve acceptability were much more frequently ignored than those necessary to achieve quality.

Vroom has designed a leadership development programme based on his normative model which will enable a manager to analyse his own decision processes against that of the model and see where he departs from the rational constraints for effective decision-making. The model proposes far greater variation for each problem situation than the typical manager exhibits. Using the model as a basis for making decisions would require such a manager to become both more autocratic *and* more participative according to the problem (cf. Fiedler, p. 191, for an opposing view on this issue).

Bibliography

Vroom, V. H., *Some Personality Determinants of the Effects of Participation,* Prentice-Hall, 1960.

Vroom, V. H., 'A New Look at Managerial Decision Making', *Organizational Dynamics* 5 (1974), 66-80.

Vroom, V. H., and Yetton, P. W., *Leadership and Decision Making,* University of Pittsburgh Press, 1973.

Michel Crozier

The distinctively French view of organizations contributed by Michel Crozier arises both from his French birth and experience and from the many periods he has spent in the United States. These periods away from France give him a perspective on his own society. He is Director of the Centre for the Sociology of Organizations in Paris, under the auspices of the Centre National de la Recherche Scientifique (CNRS), and has a long record of research in France. This has covered a wide range of organizations and administrative and social problems, but with an emphasis on studies of public administration and state-owned industries. However, his early training in sociology was in the United States, and he has spent many subsequent periods at Stanford and Harvard.

Although Crozier's view has its origins in research in France, it penetrates bureaucracies everywhere. He does not see them as monolithic rational structures, but as systems in which, despite all efforts at control, individuals and groups of individuals have room for manoeuvre. There is constant interaction between the system and the actors in the system.

This view is distinctively founded on the concept of the power *game*. An organization is seen as a series of enmeshed power games, an 'ensemble' of games. This idea is no mere colourful image. Games are very real to those in organizations. Indeed, an organization is not so much the direct creation of deliberate design as the result of the ensemble of games. The game channels power relationships and enables cooperation, reconciling the freedom of those in the organization with the constraints it places upon them.

Games are played between groups of partners of many kinds, for example between superiors and subordinates such as managers and men, or between departments and sections. The players evolve different strategies which govern what they do. Superiors may follow a strategy of 'divide and rule'; subordinates may follow a defensive strategy to protect whatever scope they may have to do things in their own way, free of interference from bosses or new regulations; occupational groups such as maintenance engineers may follow conservative (or aggressive) strategies towards technical modernization, and so on. Crozier calls this a *strategic model* of organization.

Players go so far but not too far in pursuing their strategies. Whilst each is free to gain whatever advantage can be got from a strategy rationally designed to serve his interests, the continuance of the organization is necessary for him to be able to play at all. These are not life-and-death struggles but games for position within a system, therefore limits are accepted. These are the rules of the game which players in each game must respect if it is to continue. They are not formally set-down rules, but principles which can be discovered by analysing the players' recurrent behaviour, in the same way as their strategies can be seen in what they do. There may not be complete consensus on the rules, and some players may be endeavouring to change them, but they are sufficiently acknowledged and persistent for newcomers to learn them and to absorb the associated norms and values which define acceptable and unacceptable strategies.

The players in a game are far from equal – some are more powerful than others – and their roles differ further between games, so that players who are powerful in one game may be weak in another. However, their strategies share a common fundamental objective – to gain whatever advantage is possible, within the constraining rules of the game, by restricting the choices of alternatives open to others whilst preserving or enhancing their own choices. The aim is to manoeuvre others into positions where their actions can be determined, whilst retaining one's own freedom of action. Each attempts to defend and extend his own discretion and to limit his dependence upon others, while placing them in the reverse position.

The most revealing case among those described by Crozier is that of the maintenance workers in what he terms the 'Industrial Monopoly', the French nationalized tobacco industry. At the time of Crozier's research, at the end of the 1950s and beginning of the 1960s, this was dispersed throughout the country in a large number of small and very similar factories. Each employed in the order of 350 to 400 people of which perhaps one third were direct production workers. These workers were women, and their job was to operate the semi-automatic machines turning out cigarettes, etc.

The organization was very stable, and each small factory worked in a controlled environment. Finance, raw material procurement, distribution and sales were all centrally controlled from Paris, so each local plant could get on with its task of production, unimpeded by problems. Except one. Machine stoppages.

These stoppages occurred because of breakdowns and because of variations in the tobacco leaf which required constant adjustment of machines. They were the only major happenings that could not be dealt with by impersonal bureaucratic rules or bureaucratic action from Paris. Yet if machines stopped, work stopped, and the factory stopped making what it was there for. Who could do something about it? Only the dozen or so male maintenance workers under the factory's technical engineer, who alone knew how to set and to repair the machines. No bureaucrat in Paris, no local factory director, not even the production workers on the machines, knew what they knew. They acquired the tricks of their trade from one another, and kept them to themselves. They did not explain what they did to anyone else. In their eyes it was an unforgivable sin for a production worker herself to 'fool around' with her machine which she should not touch beyond operating it in the normal way. Thus the maintenance workers succeeded in making the production workers directly, and everyone else indirectly, dependent upon them. All the others were constrained by the maintenance workers being the only ones able to deal with stoppages, whilst the maintenance workers themselves preserved their freedom of choice over what to do.

They could do so because they were powerful; and they were powerful because of their 'control over the last source of uncertainty remaining in a completely routinized organizational system'. Machine stoppages occurred unpredictably and theirs was the choice of what to do. This gave them power because those who face and cope with uncertainties have power over others who are dependent upon their choices. In the long run, power is closely related to those uncertainties on which the life of an organization depends, and the strategies of the groups in the power games are aimed at controlling the 'ultimate strategic sources of uncertainties'. *Uncertainty explains power.*

The maintenance workers therefore had power because whilst everything else was under bureaucratic control the uncertain machine stoppages were not. These had to be dealt with on the spot as they happened. They presented the maintenance workers with an opportunity which was conspicuous because it was the sole uncertainty in each factory. In other organizations the sources of uncertainty may not be so conspicuous, but in all organizations they come and go and as they do so the power of those who confront them waxes and wanes. Maintenance workers are only one example: the same applies to the rise and fall of financial experts, of production control specialists, and so on.

Why is it then that powerful experts are not able to cling to power indefinitely? If the uncertainty continues and with it their know-how they could indeed keep their grip on power, but this is unlikely because their success is self-defeating. The rationalization inherent in organizations breeds constant attempts to bring areas of uncertainty within the range of formal controls, and each expert is himself the agent of the rationalization that diminishes his own power. The more he succeeds in recording his own know-how in bureaucratic procedures and regulations, the more his own power to deal with the uncertainties himself is curtailed. His choices become restricted. Therefore the maintenance workers in the tobacco factories strove to keep their rules of thumb to themselves and to prevent them becoming bureaucratized. Even though there were officially laid down instructions for the setting and maintenance of machines kept at head office in Paris, these were completely disregarded by the maintenance workers and there were no copies in the factories themselves. For *the routinization of uncertainty removes power.*

This shapes strategies up and down hierarchies as well as between occupational groupings. The battle between superiors and subordinates involves a basic strategy by which subordinates resist rules which encroach upon their discretion, whilst pressing for rules which will limit the discretion of their superiors over them.

It is possible for opposed strategies to interlock in a series of bureaucratic vicious circles which block change. Administrators try to extend bureaucratic regulation: those subjected to it resist. The directors of the tobacco factories typically pressed for the modernization of procedures, whilst the technical engineers resisted anything that might alter the position of their maintenance workers. Crozier sees French society as a whole as an example of this, for its tendencies to bureaucratic centralization and impersonality provoke protective strategies by those affected, and these strategies in turn provoke greater bureaucratization. In every branch of administration each level of hierarchy becomes a layer protected from those above and beneath. Those beneath restrict communication to those above and stall any threatening changes, while those above make ill-informed decisions which are not carried out as intended but from the consequences of which they are shielded.

This gives rise to a peculiar rhythm of change in bureaucratic organizations, certainly in France and perhaps elsewhere too. It is an alternation of long periods of stability with very short periods of crisis and change. Conflicts are stifled until they explode. Explosive crises are therefore endemic to such bureaucracies, and necessary to them as a means for change. At such times in French bureaucracies, personal authority supersedes the rules as someone takes it upon himself to force some change out of the crisis. *Authoritarian reformer figures* wait amidst the bureaucratic routine for that moment of crisis when the system will need them.

Yet Crozier is optimistic. He hopes that if reforms were made in training and recruitment for French public administration, and in its caste system, the elites could be opened up. He argues that the large organizations of the modern world are not necessarily inimical to change, for change has never been faster and it is fastest in those societies with the largest organizations. But there is always a risk that bureaucratic structures lead to forms of power game which block the changes that are needed.

Bibliography

Crozier, M., *The Bureaucratic Phenomenon,* University of Chicago Press, 1964.

Crozier, M., and Friedberg, E., *Actors and Systems,* University of Chicago Press, 1980.

4 · *The Management of Organizations*

Scientific management will mean, for the employers and the workmen who adopt it, the elimination of almost all causes for dispute and disagreement between them.

Frederick W. Taylor

An organization does not make decisions; its function is to provide a framework, based on established criteria, within which decisions can be fashioned in an orderly manner.

Alfred P. Sloan

The needs of large-scale organization have to be satisfied by common people achieving uncommon performance.

Peter F. Drucker

I hope not for greater efficiency in our problem-solving but for better understanding of our problem-setting.

Sir Geoffrey Vickers

All managers appear to be puppets. Some decide who will pull the strings and how, and they then take advantage of each move they are forced to make. Others, unable to exploit this high-tension environment, are swallowed up by this most demanding of jobs.

Henry Mintzberg

Organizations with differing structures, functioning in different ways, have to be administered or managed. As long as there is management there will be the problem of how to manage better. In one sense, attempts at answers to the problem will be as numerous as there are managers, for each will bring his own individuality to the task. None the less, at any one time there is enough in common for there to be broad similarities in what is thought and what is taught, and for this to be widely influenced by the views of writers past and present. The writers given in this section have each sought to improve the understanding of administration and its practice. They have looked for the ingredients of a better management.

F. W. Taylor's name is synonymous with the term 'scientific management'. His ideas made him a controversial figure in his own day and have remained a subject for argument. Alfred P. Sloan, drawing on his experience as the head of the then largest corporation in the world, is concerned with establishing the management framework within which objectives are established and decisions made. Peter Drucker emphasizes the necessity of appropriate 'management by objectives', and Sir Geoffrey Vickers the combination of both fact and value which forms the managerial art of judgement. Henry Mintzberg examines the nature of the work which top managers have to do.

Frederick W. Taylor

Frederick Winslow Taylor (1856–1917) was an engineer by training. He joined the Midvale Steel Works as a labourer and rose rapidly to be foreman and later Chief Engineer. He was afterwards employed at the Bethlehem Steel Works, then became a consultant and devoted his time to the propagation of his ideas.

He first published his views on management in a paper entitled 'A piece rate system', read to the American Society of Mechanical Engineers in 1895. These views were expanded into a book *Shop Management* (1903) and further developed in *Principles of Scientific Management* (1911). As a result of labour troubles caused by the attempt to apply his principles in a government arsenal, a House of Representatives' Special Committee was set up in 1911 to investigate Taylor's system of shop management. (A full description of events at the arsenal is given in Aitken's case study.) In 1947, *Shop Management*, the *Principles*, and Taylor's Testimony to the Special Committee were collected together and published under the title of *Scientific Management*.

Taylor was the founder of the movement known as 'scientific management'. 'The principal object of management', he states, 'should be to secure the maximum prosperity for the employer, coupled with the maximum prosperity of each employee.' For the employer, 'maximum prosperity' means not just large profits in the short term but the development of all aspects of the enterprise to a state of permanent prosperity. For the employee 'maximum prosperity' means not just immediate higher wages, but his development so that he may perform efficiently in the highest grade of work for which his natural abilities fit him. The mutual interdependence of management and workers, and the necessity of their working together towards the common aim of increased prosperity for all seemed completely self-evident to Taylor. He was thus driven to asking: Why is there so much antagonism and inefficiency?

He suggests three causes: first, the fallacious belief of the workers that any increase in output would inevitably result in unemployment; second, the defective systems of management which make it necessary for each worker to restrict his output in order to protect his interests ('systematic soldiering'); third, inefficient rule-of-thumb effort-wasting methods of work. Taylor conceived it to be the aim of 'scientific management' to overcome these obstacles. This could be achieved by a systematic study of work to discover the most efficient methods of performing the job, and then a systematic study of management leading to the most efficient methods of controlling the workers. This would bring a great increase in efficiency and with it prosperity to the benefit of all, since a highly efficient prosperous business would be in a much better position to ensure the continuing well-paid employment of its workers. As Taylor put it: 'What the workmen want from their employers beyond anything else is high wages and what employers want from their workmen most of all is low labour cost of manufacture ... the existence or absence of these two elements forms the best index to either good or bad management.'

To achieve this Taylor lays down four 'great underlying principles of management':

The development of a true science of work

He points out that we do not really know what constitutes a fair day's work; a boss therefore has unlimited opportunities for complaining about his workers' inadequacies, and a worker never really knows what is expected of him. This can be remedied by the establishment after scientific investigation of a 'large daily task' as the amount to be done by a suitable worker under optimum conditions. For this he would receive a high rate of pay – much higher than the average worker would receive in 'unscientific' factories. He would also suffer a loss of income if he failed to achieve this performance.

The scientific selection and progressive development of the workman

To earn this high rate of pay a workman would have to be scientifically selected to ensure that he possesses the physical and intellectual qualities to enable him to achieve the output. Then he must be systematically trained to be a 'first-class' man. Taylor believes that every worker could be a first-class man at some job. It was the responsibility of management to develop workers, offering them opportunities for advancement which would finally enable them to do 'the highest, most interesting and most profitable class of work' for which they could become 'first-class' men.

The bringing together of the science of work and the scientifically selected and trained men

It is this process that causes the 'mental revolution' in management and Taylor maintains that almost invariably the major resistance to scientific management comes from the side of management. The workers, he finds, are very willing to cooperate in learning to do a good job for a high rate of pay.

The constant and intimate cooperation of management and men

There is an almost equal division of work and responsibility between management and workers. The management take over all the work for which they are better fitted than the workmen, i.e. the specification and verification of the methods, time, price and quality standards of the job, and the continuous supervision and control of the worker doing it. 'There is hardly a single act ... done by any workman in the shop which is not preceded by and followed by some act on the part of the men in management.' With this close personal cooperation the opportunities for conflict are almost eliminated, since the operation of this authority is not arbitrary. The manager is continually demonstrating that his decisions are subject to the same discipline as the workmen, namely the scientific study of the work.

By 'science' Taylor means systematic observation and measurement, and an example of his method that he often quotes is the development of 'the science of shovelling'. He is insistent that, although shovelling is a very simple job, the study of the factors affecting efficient shovelling is quite complex. So much so that a man who is phlegmatic enough to be able to do the job and stupid enough to choose it is extremely unlikely to be able to develop the most efficient method by himself. But this is in fact what is hoped will happen. The *scientific* study of shovelling involves the determination of the optimum load that a 'first-class man' can handle with each shovelful. Then the correct size of shovel to obtain this load, with different materials, must be established. Workers must be provided with a range of shovels and told which one to use. They must then be placed on an incentive payment scheme which allows first-class men to earn high wages (double what they would earn in 'unscientific' firms) in return for high production.

The insistence on maximum specialization, and the removal of all extraneous elements in order to concentrate on the essential task, is fundamental to Taylor's thinking. He applies this concept to management too. He considers that the work of a typical factory foreman is composed of a number of different functions (such as cost clerk, time clerk, inspector, repair boss, shop disciplinarian) and he believes that these could be separated out and performed by different specialists who would each be responsible for controlling different aspects of the work and the workers. He calls this system 'functional management' and likens the increased efficiency that it would bring to that obtained in a school where classes go to specialist teachers for different subjects, compared with a school in which one teacher teaches all subjects. He also formulates 'the exception principle' which lays down that management reports should be condensed into comparative summaries giving in detail only the exceptions to past standards or averages – both the especially good and the especially bad exceptions. Thus the manager would obtain an immediate and comprehensive view of the progress of his shop.

Taylor's methods have been followed by many others, among them Gantt, Frank and Lillian Gilbreth, Bedaux, Rowan and Halsey. They have developed his thinking into what is now called Work Study, or sometimes Industrial Engineering, a wider term. But even in his lifetime Taylor's ideas led to bitter controversy over the alleged inhumanity of his system, which was said to reduce men to the level of efficiently functioning machines. In fairness to Taylor, it must be said that his principles were often inadequately understood. For example, few managements have been willing to put into practice one of his basic tenets – that there should be no limit to the earnings of a high-producing worker; many incentive schemes involve such limits. This may inhibit the 'mental revolution' Taylor sought, which requires that 'both sides take their eyes off the division of the surplus as the all important matter and together turn their attention towards increasing the size of the surplus'.

Bibliography

Taylor, F. W., *Scientific Management*, Harper & Row, 1947.
Aitken, H. G. J., *Taylorism at Watertown Arsenal*, Harvard University Press, 1960.

Alfred P. Sloan

Alfred Sloan (1875–1966) spent forty-five years in the General Motors Corporation of America, then the largest industrial corporation in the world. For twenty-three of those years, from 1923 until 1946, he was the chief executive officer of the Corporation and he continued as Chairman of the Board until 1956. As such he was the person with the greatest influence on the way in which General Motors developed. He was largely responsible for the creation of the present form of the organization and of the methods of its top management, and through this achievement has had a considerable influence on the methods of management of many large industrial and other enterprises, whose developments are analysed by Chandler (p. 50).

Sloan, an engineer by training, was the epitome of the professional manager. In this he contrasted very strongly with the founder of General Motors, William Durant, who had a highly personal style of management akin to his great rival in the American motor industry, Henry Ford. Durant was a genius at creating enterprises but was much less capable of carrying them on, and a bankers' trust and later the du Pont Company acquired control before General Motors became financially independent. Sloan, on the other hand, although he had a considerable fortune by personal standards (now administered by the Sloan Foundation), never at its greatest owned more than one per cent of the stock of the Corporation. He was thus in Weber's terms (see p. 15) the bureaucratic administrator who succeeded the charismatic founder. In 1963 Sloan published *My Years with General Motors* in which he gave a history of the top management problems of the Corporation and his methods of handling them. In this he demonstrated the way in which the technical, financial, organizational and personal factors interact in the management of large enterprises.

The recurrent theme of Sloan's book is the necessity of dealing with the major problem which faces any large multi-operation enterprise: the appropriate degree of centralization or decentralization of authority for decisions. The centralizing approach has the advantages of flexibility and perhaps speed, but places an enormous weight on the top man. He may be a genius in many of his decisions, but he will also be haphazard, irrational and apathetic in regard to others. This was the Henry Ford approach. The decentralizing approach has the advantage of allowing decisions to be made closer to the operational bases of the enterprise, but runs the real danger that decisions will be taken with regard to the best interests of the particular operating division itself without concern for the best interests of the corporation as a whole. This was the William Durant method. He brought many companies into the General Motors Corporation (including the roller bearing company owned by Sloan) and allowed their managements to operate much as before with little regard to the rather nebulous concept of the corporation as a whole. The management history of General Motors is one of the attempt to find the right balance between these two extremes, in an industrial environment of constant change and continuous, but fluctuating, growth.

A nice example of the extreme decentralization in the early days is the description given by Sloan of the method of cash control. Each operating unit controlled its own cash, depositing all receipts in its own accounts and paying all bills from them. There was no income directly to the Corporation and no effective procedure for getting cash from the points where it happened to be to the points where it was needed. When the Corporation needed cash to pay dividends, taxes and other charges, the treasurer had to request cash from the operating divisions. But the divisions wanted to keep as much cash as possible to satisfy their own peak requirements, and their financial staff were highly adept at delaying the reporting of cash in hand. The treasurer would thus have to guess how much cash a division had in hand and decide how much of this he would try to get from them. He would visit them, discuss other general matters and then casually at the end of the conversation bring up the topic of cash. The division would always express surprise at the amount that he wanted, and occasionally would try to resist the transfer of such a large amount. The effects of this bargaining situation were that over the Corporation as a whole funds were not efficiently utilized, and so a centralized cash control system was set up. General Motors Corporation accounts were established and controlled by the central finance staff; all receipts were credited to them and all payments made from them. Transfers between one account and another could be made quickly and easily across the whole country when cash needed in one place was available in another. Minimum and maximum balances for each local account were set, inter-corporation settlements were facilitated, and forward planning of cash was developed, all by the central staff.

So centralization can clearly bring great advantages, and systems of coordination for purchasing, corporate advertising, engineering and so on were set up. But there is also a clear need for decentralization if the central directing staff is not to stifle the division managements. The controversy over the 'copper-cooled engine' which rent the Corporation in the early nineteen-twenties well illustrates this. The research section of the central staff had developed a revolutionary air-cooled engine and with the strong backing of the then Chairman, Pierre du Pont, was pressing that all production should be turned over to this type. The operating divisions were resistant since they regarded the development as unproven on a production and use basis. Sloan did not regard himself as technically competent to take a view on the merits of the engine, but from a purely managerial analysis he came to the conclusion that for the central direction of the corporation to force the change on unwilling division managements would be in effect for them to undertake the operating management of the divisions – a degree of centralization which was inappropriate and basically unworkable. He therefore threw his weight in support of the divisions, proposing that a special subsidiary of the research division be formed to develop and manufacture cars based on the new engine. This was done, and, although the development eventually proved unworkable with the engineering technology of those days, the Corporation learnt a great deal from this controversy about the correct balance between the centre and the divisions.

Top management, according to Sloan, has the basic tasks of providing motivation and opportunity for its senior executives; motivation by incentive compensation through stock option plans, and opportunity through decentralized management. But co-ordination is also required, and good management rests on a recon-ciliation of centralization and decentralization. It was through his attempts to obtain the correct structural balance between these extremes that Sloan enunciated his seemingly paradoxical principle of 'coordinated decentralization'. His aim was coordinated control of decentralized operations. Policy coordination is achieved through committees. It is evolved in a continuous debate to which all may contribute, and is basically an educational process. Executive administration is the clear responsibility of individuals who carry out the evolving policy. Many policy groups were established in the Corporation, but none of them detracted from the executive functions – indeed they are the means of controlling them.

For such a system of coordinated control of decentralized operations to work, one further element is needed – committees have to be supplied with adequate facts on which to base policies, and executive management has to be based on fact. Time and time again throughout his tenure of office Sloan emphasized this; debates are being conducted on conjectures, decisions are taken on superficial evidence, only inadequate information is available and improved systems must be developed to correct this. Through his influence General Motors pioneered many new techniques for obtaining managerially relevant information, particularly in financial control through the use of return on capital as a measure of efficiency, and in the statistical forecasting of market demand.

Bibliography

Sloan, A. P., *My Years with General Motors,* New York: Doubleday, 1964.

Peter F. Drucker

Peter Drucker was born in Austria. He qualified in law and was a journalist in Germany until the advent of the Nazis. After a period in London, he moved to New York in 1937. He has been an economic consultant to banks and insurance companies and an adviser on business policy and management to a large number of American corporations. His many books on business topics have made him one of the leading contemporary writers on management policy issues. He was for many years at New York University Business School and since 1971 has been Clarke Professor of Social Science at Claremont Graduate School, California.

Drucker's work begins with a view of top management and its critical role in the representative institution of modern industrial society, namely the large corporation. Following from this he identifies management as the central problem area, and the manager as the dynamic element in every business. It is the manager through his control of the decision-making structure of the modern corporation who breathes life into the organization and the society. The manager is given human and material resources to work with, and from them he fashions a productive enterprise from which springs the wealth of the society. This is becoming increasingly true as we move into an era of knowledge technology, making human resources ever more central to effective performance in organizations. Yet as Drucker points out, managers, while becoming ever more basic resources of a business, are increasingly the scarcest, the most expensive and the most perishable. Given this, it becomes extremely important that managers should be used as effectively as is possible at the present state of knowledge about the practice and functions of management. It is to the problem of managerial effectiveness that Drucker addresses himself.

It is only possible to arrive at prescriptions for effectiveness if we first understand the role of the manager in the organization; if we know what the job of management is. There are, says Drucker, two dimensions to the task of management, an economic dimension and a time dimension. Managers are responsible for business organizations (this distinguishes them from administrators generally). As such they must always put economic performance first; the final standard for judging them is economic performance, which of course is not the case for all administrators. The second dimension, time, is one which is present in all decision-making systems. Management always has to think of the impact of a decision on the present, the short term future and the long term future. This is, of course, tied in with the economic aspect. Taken together it means that managers are evaluated in terms of their economic performance in the present, the short term and the long term.

Management, then, is the job of organizing resources to achieve satisfactory performance; to produce an enterprise from material and human resources. According to Drucker this does not necessarily mean profit maximization. For him profit is not the cause of business behaviour, or the rationale of business decision-making in the sense of always attempting to achieve the maximum profit. Rather profit is a test of the validity or success of the business enterprise. The aim of any business is to achieve sufficient profit, which will cover the risks that have been taken and avoid a loss.

The central question for Drucker is how best to manage a business to ensure that profits are made, and that the enterprise is successful over time. Although it is possible to state the overall aims in a fairly precise and simple way, any on-going functioning organization has a variety of needs and goals. It is not realistic to think of an enterprise having a single objective. Efficient management always involves a juggling act, balancing the different possible objectives, deciding the priorities to be put on the multiple aims that an organization has. Because of this, and due to the complex nature of business as exemplified by departmentalization, management by objectives is vital. This is essential in the process of ensuring that informed judgement takes place. It forces managers to examine available alternatives and provides a reliable means for evaluating management performance.

Specifically, objectives in a business enterprise enable management to explain, predict and control activities in a way which single ideas like profit maximization do not. First, they enable the organization to explain the whole range of business phenomena in a small number of general statements. Secondly, they allow the testing of these statements in actual experience. Thirdly, it becomes possible to predict behaviour. Fourthly, the soundness of decisions can be examined while they are still being made rather than after the fact. Fifthly, performance in the future can be improved as a result of the analysis of past experience. This is because objectives force one to plan in detail what the business must aim at and to work out ways of effectively achieving these aims. Management by objectives involves spelling out what is meant by managing a business. By doing this, and then examining the outcome over time the five advantages outlined above are realized.

But this still leaves the problem of what the objectives of a business enterprise should be. To quote Drucker: 'Objectives are needed in every area where performance and results directly and vitally affect the survival and prosperity of the business.' More concretely, there are eight areas in business where performance objectives must be set. These areas are: market standing; innovation; productivity; physical and financial resources; profitability; manager performance and development; worker performance and attitude; public responsibility. In deciding how to set objectives for these areas it is necessary to take account of possible measures and lay down a realistic time span. Measures are important because they make things visible and 'real'; they tell the manager what to focus his attention upon. Unfortunately measurement in most areas of business is still at a very crude level. As far as the time span of objectives is concerned, this depends on the area and the nature of the business. In the lumber business, today's plantings are the production capacity of fifty years' time; in parts of the clothing industry a few weeks' time may be the 'long-range future'.

But perhaps the most important part of management by objectives is the effect that it has on the manager himself. It enables the organization to develop its most important resource, management. This is because managerial self-control is developed, leading to stronger motivation and more efficient learning. It is the essence of this style of management that each manager arrives at a set of realistic objectives for the unit which he controls, and for himself. These objectives should spell out the contribution that the manager will make to the attainment of company goals in all areas of the business. It is always necessary that the objectives set should be checked by higher levels of management to make sure that they are attainable (neither too high nor too low). But the importance of individual managerial involvement in the setting of objectives cannot be overstressed as a motivator. If the manager is really going to be able to develop himself in performance terms and take proper advantage of the system, he must be given information direct which will enable him to measure his own performance. This is very different from the situation in some companies where certain groups (e.g. accountants) act as the 'secret police' of the chief executive.

The necessity of individual managers setting their own objectives stems from the nature of modern business, and what Drucker calls three forces of misdirection. These are: the specialized work of most managers, the existence of a hierarchy, and the differences in vision that exist in businesses. All these raise the possibility of breakdown and conflicts in the organization. Management by objectives is a way of overcoming these deficiencies by relating the task of each manager to the overall goals of the company. By doing this it takes note of an important aspect of modern business operations; management is no longer the domain of one man. Even the chief executive does not operate in isolation. Management is a group operation, and the existence of objectives emphasizes the contribution that each individual manager makes to the total group operation. The problem of a chief executive is that of picking the best managerial group; the existence of objectives with their built-in evaluation system enables better choices to be made.

Management by objectives, then, enables an executive to be effective. An important point is that effectiveness can be learned. Drucker insists that the self-development of effective executives is central to the continued development of the organization as the 'knowledge worker' becomes the major resource. The system of objectives allows the manager to evaluate his performance and by so doing strengthens the learning process. This is done by showing where the particular strengths of the individual are, as a result of which he can make these strengths productive by demonstrating the correctness of different systems of priorities, and by producing effective decision-making patterns. The regular review of objectives and performance enables the manager to know where his most effective contribution is made, how it is made, and as a result develop his skills in these areas.

Overall then, management by objectives helps to overcome some of the forces which threaten to split the organization, by clearly relating the task of each manager to the overall aims of the company. It allows learning to take place and as a result the development of each manager to the best of his capacities. And finally, and most important, it increases the motivation of the managers and develops their commitment to the organization. The result is that organizational goals are reached by having common people achieve uncommon performance.

Bibliography

Drucker, P. F., *The Practice of Management,* Harper & Row, 1954.
Drucker, P. F., *Managing for Results,* Harper & Row, 1964.
Drucker, P. F., *The Effective Executive,* Harper & Row, 1966.
Drucker, P. F., *The Unseen Revolution,* Harper & Row, 1976.
Drucker, P. F., *Managing in Turbulent Times,* Harper & Row, 1980.

Sir Geoffrey Vickers

Sir Geoffrey Vickers (1894–1982) served in the First World War, and was awarded the Victoria Cross for bravery. He worked as a solicitor and then took charge during the Second World War of British economic intelligence. He was knighted in 1946 and then became the member of the National Coal Board in charge of manpower, education, health and welfare. It was in the last twenty years or so of his life that he developed, systematized and recorded his ideas about institutions, organizations and policy-making. At his death in his eighty-eighth year, he was visiting Professor of Systems at the University of Lancaster and still engaged on fresh work.

The processes of policy-making, decision-making and control are at the centre of Vickers's analysis. All of these processes take place within an organized setting – a group, an organization, an institution or a society. They are the key to understanding how organizations actually work.

Much of Vickers's extensive writing derives from his principal concern with the idea of *regulation*. Regulation is essentially the process of ensuring that any system follows the path that has been set for it. It is a concept that derives from information theory, systems theory, cybernetics and the control of machines. Vickers used ideas deriving primarily from technological contexts as a basis for developing a whole range of analytical concepts about policy-making and management.

If one is to ensure that an organization is to carry out the functions and activities specified by its controllers, a number of activities have to happen which, taken together, constitute the regulation of a system. First, it is necessary for the controllers (the managers) to establish what the state of the system is, to find out what is happening. For Vickers this involves making what he calls *reality judgements*, establishing the facts. But facts do not have an independent meaning; their significance has to be judged. This involves the second part of the process of regulation, namely, making a *value judgement*. This can only be done by comparing the actual state of an organization with a standard which acts as a norm. The third part of the process involves devising the means to reduce any disparity between the norm and actuality. Taken together these three elements make up the regulative process of information, valuation and action.

It may initially sound as though regulation is a mechanical process, but this would be far from the truth. While the basic ideas come from machine systems Vickers is very clear that adaptations and additions are necessary when it comes to the management of organizations and other human systems. The making of judgements is a uniquely human function which he describes as an art (see *The Art of Judgement*). Central to making judgements is the process of *appreciation* because judgements involve the selection of information, the application of values and the choice of action. None of these processes is self-evident or straightforward. Any manager facing a situation has to make an appreciation of it. This is true not just of arriving at standards, but also of collecting information. Appreciation involves the manager in making choices and selections; deciding what indicators to use to describe the state of the organization; choosing what standards to set and what courses of action to follow. Appreciation requires the specifically human capacity of a readiness to see and value objects and situations in one way rather than another.

There is a very important relationship between regulation and appreciation. To regulate (control), the regulator (manager) has to deal with a series of variables, elements of a situation which establish how well a system (organization) is performing. But a manager can only deal with a limited number of such variables. Which variables are chosen for the purpose of regulation is a function of a manager's appreciative system. Like Herbert Simon (p. 104) on whose work he draws, Vickers points out that there are cognitive limits to what an individual can handle, the amount that he can usefully watch and regulate. A manager is also limited by his interests in the selection of variables to attend to. Cognition and interests are elements in his appreciative system.

Appreciation has a major role to play in organizational and institutional management because it steers the judgements that controllers make by setting the system. Because it is through his appreciative system that a manager makes both his reality and value judgements, such a system sets the limits to what are to be regarded as choices and what as constraining. This steering function establishes what is enabling, what is limiting and what is crucial. The basic policy choice in any organization is what to regard as regulatable, and the choice made lays down what the key relations and central norms of the system are to be.

Having established the central analytical constructs of regulation and appreciation and their relationship to one another, much of Vickers's work is then concerned with integrating a psychologically based approach to control, emphasizing individual characteristics, with further analysis which places the controller in a collective setting. Managers have to operate with and through others; the process of regulation is not machine-like for human systems. This means that choice and action have to be organized and operated on a collective basis. For this to happen there has to be a set of shared understandings, an agreed set of norms.

The manager, through his organizational position and appreciative system, has a key role in both building up the general appreciative setting of his organization through which organizational members establish common ways of operating, and also in setting up communication systems to deal with disparities that arise. It is a central issue for a manager to cope with the fact that shared norms, shared understandings and shared communication cannot be taken for granted. Indeed, Vickers suggests that control and regulation in organizations and institutions are becoming more problematic precisely because of the difficulty of maintaining agreement. This is because, on the one hand, there is a continuing escalation of expectations and organizations which reflect this attempt to try and regulate more and more relations. On the other hand, the capacity of individuals for accepting regulation is steadily being eroded with the evaporation of loyalty to organizations and the growing emphasis on *individual* self-realization (of which Vickers is highly critical). Together these produce a paradox for the contemporary manager, dealing with employees and clients who are at one and the same time highly *dependent* and very *alienated*.

Attempting to deal with this paradox brings the wheel full circle to the importance of the appreciative system of the manager. This is because it is his appreciative system which determines how the issues will be seen and defined and what action will be taken. The manager is involved in making choices which are problematic because they are multi-valued. Choices are not simple and straight-forward, they require the assessment of a number of dimensions which can be valued in a variety of ways. To regulate this involves the ability to predict possible outcomes and to learn about the relationship between action and outcomes.

The ability to deal with the paradox and so to regulate an organizational and institutional system is limited by the nature of what is changing. The rate and predictability of regulatable change sets limits to what is regulatable. To regulate an organization, the variables which the appreciative system regards as key in evaluating performance have to be predicted over time. Indeed, such variables need to be predicted over a time period at least as long as the time needed to make an effective response. Part of the reason for the breakdown of confidence in institutions derives from the fact that rates of change are high, shared understandings of what they mean and why they occur are difficult to establish, the prediction of future action is extremely problematic.

In the end, it is the manager with his appreciative system operating in a particular setting who carries out control and regulation. He helps to set, and is affected by, what are regarded as standards of success, what scope of discretion is allowed and what is the extent of power. Crucial to the operation is what is regarded as possible. It is necessary for those responsible for control to constantly examine how they appreciate the world, to test the limits of their logic and skill and to always be open to new ideas. Learn-ing is control because of the role of appreciation in regulation.

Bibliography

Vickers, Sir G., *The Art of Judgement,* New York: Basic Books, 1965.
Vickers, Sir G., *Towards a Sociology of Management,* New York: Basic Books, 1967.
Vickers, Sir G., *Value Systems and Social Process,* London: Tavistock Publications, 1968.
Vickers, Sir G., *Making Institutions Work,* New York: Halsted Press, 1973.

Henry Mintzberg

Henry Mintzberg is a professor of management policy at McGill University, Montreal. He graduated from the Sloan School of Management at the Massachusetts Institute of Technology. He has been a visiting professor at the University of Aix-en-Provence in France. He has also acted as a consultant to a number of organizations, working on issues of policy, structure and operations. His interests in research, consultancy and writing have constantly been focused on tying together a wide range of organizational issues.

There are a number of strands to the ideas of Mintzberg, including the nature of decision-making, types of organizational structure and functioning and what managers' jobs actually involve. It is in this latter area that he has made a particular contribution to our understanding of how organizations work, a contribution which has been important to both practising managers and academic students of management. But the thrust of his approach is always to understand the reality and actuality of organizations.

Mintzberg's approach to what managers actually do arose from a realization that nobody really knew. He is at pains to distinguish between the many prescriptions about what managers *ought* to do and the extent to which there is any adequate *description* of a manager's job. His starting point is to review eight schools of thought on the manager's job and to find them wanting. These eight schools he identifies as: the Classical; the Great Man; the Entrepreneurship; the Decision Theory; the Leader Effectiveness; the Leader Power; the Leader Behaviour; and the Work Activity.

The Classical school is based on POSDCORB, the idea derived from the initial analysis of Fayol (p. 64) that managers Plan, Organize, Staff, Direct, Coordinate, Report and Budget. It is very influential and highly prescriptive. The Great Man school is almost the opposite of POSDCORB suggesting that the work of managers can be best understood by looking at what leading exponents said they did. Unlike the Classical school it does not attempt to produce general principles. The Entrepreneurship school is derived from economics, stressing the role of the manager as rational decision-maker, in particular producing innovative new combinations of activities. The Decision Theory school criticizes the entrepreneurial approach by stressing the limitations on rational decision-making and the differences between programmed and unprogrammed decisions (cf. Simon, p. 104 and Lindblom, p. 114).

The Leader Effectiveness school focuses on the idea of the manager as leader and most attention has been centred on the distinction between autocratic and participative styles (cf. Likert and McGregor, p. 164). The Leader Power school deals with the politics of interpersonal behaviour, looking at sources of power. The Leader Behaviour school is one of the few approaches which has actually studied what managers do. Because of the wide range of concerns exhibited by the writers Mintzberg includes under this category, it is difficult to say what they have in common other than the study of behaviour. This approach is also shown in Mintzberg's final school, the Work Activity school, which is concerned with the systematic analysis of managers' activities. These last two schools are at the furthest extreme from POSDCORB.

For Mintzberg, none of these schools is at all adequate in describing the work of a manager, although taken together they may provide a starting point. To really get to grips with what managers actually do, as opposed to what they might or should do, four aspects have to be dealt with. These are job characteristics, job content, job variations and job programming.

It is in outlining job characteristics that Mintzberg demonstrates the greatest difference between what managers do and what they are said to do. On the basis of work activity studies he demonstrates that a manager's job is characterized by pace, interruptions, brevity, variety and fragmentation of activities and a preference for verbal contacts. He spends a considerable amount of time in scheduled meetings and acts as an important point in networks of contacts. Such a picture raises the question of what control a manager might exercise over his activities. Control may come from a few critical decisions which determine long-term activities and roles and by seizing opportunities from situations in which he must take part.

The fragmentary nature of a manager's activity leads to the suggestion that he actually has to perform a wide variety of roles, something which is reflected in the pattern of activities. However,

Mintzberg suggests that this variety can be grouped into three areas covering ten roles. The areas are *interpersonal, informational, decisional.*

Naturally, interpersonal roles cover the relationships that a manager has to have with others. The three roles within this category are figurehead, leader and liaison. A manager has to act as a *figurehead*, because of his formal authority and symbolic position; there are activities and situations in which he has to act as the representative of his organization. As a *leader*, a manager has to create climates and bring together the needs of an organization and those of the individuals under his command. He can do this through the exercise of managerial power. The third interpersonal role, that of *liaison*, deals with the horizontal relationship which work-activity studies have shown to be important for a manager. A manager has to maintain a network of relationships with others outside his particular organization.

With their position in an organization, managers have to collect, transmit and disseminate information: it is this position that underscores the set of informational roles, namely monitor, disseminator and spokesman. A manager is an important figure in *monitoring* what goes on in his organization, and around him, receiving information about both internal and external events, and transmitting it to others. This process of transmission is the *dissemination* role, passing on information of both a factual and value kind, to others in his organization. Because of his position a manager often has to provide information concerning his organization to outsiders. It is this activity which constitutes the role of *spokesman*. He has to deal with both the general public and those in specific positions of influence.

As with so many writers about management, Mintzberg regards the most crucial part of managerial activity as that concerned with making various kinds of decisions. The four roles that he places in this category are based on different classes of decision, namely, entrepreneur, disturbance handler, resource allocator and negotiator. As an *entrepreneur* a manager is exercising his capacity to make decisions about changing what is happening in an organization. He may have to both initiate change and take an active role in the design process. In principle, in such a decision situation, a manager is acting voluntarily, deciding to introduce a change process. This is very different from his actions as a *disturbance handler* where a manager has to make decisions which arise as a result of events which may be beyond his control and unpredicted. The ability to react to events as well as to plan activities is an important managerial skill in Mintzberg's eyes.

The *resource allocation* role of a manager is central to much organizational analysis. Clearly a manager has to make decisions about the allocation of money, people, equipment, time and so on. Mintzberg takes an important step beyond this statement to point out that in allocating resources a manager is actually scheduling time, programming work and authorizing actions. The *negotiation* role is put in the decisional category by Mintzberg because it is 'resource trading in real time'. A manager has to negotiate with others and in the process be able to make decisions about the commitment of organizational resources.

For Mintzberg these ten roles provide a more adequate description of what managers do than any of the various schools of management thought. In these roles it is information that is crucial; the manager is a processor of information priority. Through his interpersonal roles a manager ensures that he is provided with information; by means of the decisional roles information is used. It is information that is the linch pin.

Of course, the roles that define a manager's work can be put together in a variety of ways by any particular manager. Because Mintzberg is concerned with describing, not prescribing, he suggests that what a manager actually does is contingent upon the person that he is, the situation he is in, the kind of job he does and the general environment in which all of this takes place. Under the constraints of these factors any particular manager chooses to exercise some roles rather than others. On the basis of the key roles emphasized, Mintzberg says there are eight managerial job types which emerge. The titles of these are largely self-explanatory, namely, contact man, political manager, entrepreneur, insider, real-time manager, team manager, expert manager and new manager.

From these various ways of describing and summarizing what managers do, a number of central points emerge for Mintzberg. One is that management is not reducible to a set of scientific statements and programmes, rigorously tested and available to be followed. While there is scope for extending the work of management science into the field of policy-making and supervision, enough is not yet known to think of management as a profession based on a scientific discipline. A further point, related to the first, is that the manager is caught in a task which is highlighted by brevity, fragmentation and superficiality. It is paradoxical that it is these characteristics that make it difficult to introduce improved working practices. This is the 'managerial loop'. Another point concerns the kinds of 'prescriptions' that Mintzberg is prepared to make. Because for him management is essentially an art, it is necessary for a manager to try and learn continuously about his own situation. Self-study is vital and is currently the only way for a manager to improve his performance. At the moment there is no solid basis for teaching a theory of managing. According to Mintzberg 'the management school has been more effective at training technocrats to deal with structured problems than managers to deal with unstructured ones'.

This latter point is important to understanding Mintzberg's later work on decision-making and the structuring of organizations. He points out the complexity of decision-making and the fact that many steps are involved, in an iterative way, and indicates that deciding on a course of action is but a small part of the process. There is a great deal that is unstructured about decision-making. A further theme in Mintzberg's work is the complexity of organizations. This leads him to suggest five structural configurations, different organizational forms. These are Simple Structure, Machine Bureaucracy, Professional Bureaucracy, Divisionalized Form and Autocracy. These structures are based on different patterns of elements such as the nature of coordination, the groups that control and the type of decision-making. Each type is adapted to different situations.

Mintzberg's ideas and work on managers, decisions and structures, together underline the unstructured nature of much that happens in organizations, the complexity of organizational operation, the need for adaptive patterns of operation and the necessity for writers on organizations to deal with the reality of management.

Bibliography

Mintzberg, H., *The Nature of Managerial Work,* Harper & Row, 1973.
Mintzberg, H., *The Structuring of Organizations,* Prentice-Hall, 1979.

5 · *People in Organizations*

Management succeeds or fails in proportion as it is accepted without reservation by the group as authority and leader.

Elton Mayo

The entire organization must consist of a multiple overlapping group structure with *every* work group using group decision-making processes skilfully.

Rensis Likert

The average human being learns, under proper conditions, not only to accept but to seek responsibility.

Douglas McGregor

The 9, 9 orientation to the management of production and people aims at integrating these two aspects of work under conditions of high concern for both.

R. R. Blake and J. S. Mouton

It is my hypothesis that the present organizational strategies developed and used by administrators (be they industrial, educational, religious, governmental or trade union) lead to human and organizational decay. It is also my hypothesis that this need not be so.

Chris Argyris

The primary functions of any organization, whether religious, political or industrial, should be to implement the needs of man to enjoy a meaningful existence.

Frederick Herzberg

The closest approximation to the all round good leader is likely to be the individual who intuitively or through training knows how to manage his environment so that the leadership situation best matches his leadership style.

F. E. Fiedler

Psycho-economic equilibrium is best achieved in the individual by a level of work corresponding to his capacity, and equitable payment for that work.

Elliott Jaques

As society changes, so must its organizations; as organizations change, so must their pay systems.

E. E. Lawler

Organizations are systems of interdependent *human beings*. Although this has been recognized implicitly by many of the writers of the previous chapters, and explicitly by some, their main concern has been with the 'formal system' – its aims, the principles on which it should be constituted to achieve them, and the methods by which it should function. People have then been considered as one of the essential resources required to achieve the aims. But people are a rather special sort of resource. They not only work for the organization – they *are* the organization.

The behaviour of the members of an organization clearly affects both its structure and its functioning, as well as the principles on which it can be managed. Most importantly, human beings affect the aims of organizations in which they participate – not merely the methods used to accomplish them. The writers in this chapter are social scientists who are specifically concerned to analyse the behaviour of people and its effects on all aspects of the organization. They have studied human attitudes, expectations, value systems, tensions and conflicts and the effects these have on productivity, adaptability, cohesion and morale. They have regarded the organization as a 'natural system' – an organism whose processes have to be studied in their own right – rather than as a 'formal system' – a mechanism designed to achieve particular ends.

Elton Mayo is the founding father of the 'Human Relations Movement' which brought into prominence the view that workers and managers must first be understood as human beings. Rensis Likert and Douglas McGregor reject the underlying assumptions about human behaviour on which formal organizations have been built and propose new methods of management based on a more adequate understanding of human motivation, while Robert Blake and Jane Mouton describe a form of management which shows equal high concern for both production and people.

Chris Argyris has been concerned to examine and control the inevitable conflict between the needs of the individual and the needs of the organization, and Frederick Herzberg to determine how the characteristically human needs of man for growth and development may be satisfied in work.

Fred Fiedler analyses appropriate styles of leadership for effectiveness in differing situations. Elliott Jaques has focused upon the problems of tension and reducing them through adequate role definition; both he and Edward Lawler examine the impact on the individual of inequitable payment systems.

Elton Mayo and
the Hawthorne Investigations

Elton Mayo (1880–1949) was an Australian who spent most of his working life at Harvard University, eventually becoming Professor of Industrial Research in the Graduate School of Business Administration. In this post he was responsible for the initiation and direction of many research projects, the most famous being the five-year investigation of the Hawthorne works of the Western Electric Company in Chicago. Immediately prior to his death, Mayo was consultant on industrial problems to the British Government.

Elton Mayo has often been called the founder of both the Human Relations movement and of industrial sociology. The research that he directed showed the importance of groups in affecting the behaviour of individuals at work and enabled him to make certain deductions about what managers ought to do.

Like most of his contemporaries, Mayo's initial interests were in fatigue, accidents and labour turnover, and the effect on these of rest pauses and physical conditions of work. One of his first investigations was of a spinning mill in Philadelphia where labour turnover in one department was 250 per cent compared with an average of 6 per cent for all the other departments. Rest pauses were introduced by Mayo and production and morale improved. When the operatives took part in fixing the frequency and duration of the pauses a further improvement was registered and morale in the whole factory also improved. At the end of the first year, turnover in the department concerned was down to the average for the rest of the mill. The initial explanation was that the rest pauses, in breaking up the monotony of the job, improved the mental and physical condition of the men. However, after subsequent investigations, Mayo modified his explanation.

The major investigation which led to this modification and which laid the basis for a great many subsequent studies was the Hawthorne Experiment carried out between 1927 and 1932. Prior to the entry of Mayo's team an inquiry had been made by a number of engineers into the effect of illumination on the worker and his work.

Two groups of workers had been isolated and the lighting conditions for one had been varied and for the other held constant. No significant differences in output were found between the two; indeed whatever was done with the lighting, production rose in *both* groups.

At this point the Industrial Research team directed by Mayo took over. The first stage of their inquiry is known as the Relay Assembly Test Room. Six female operatives, engaged in assembling telephone relays, were segregated in order to observe the effect on output and morale of various changes in the conditions of work. During the five years of experiment various changes were introduced and a continuous record of output was kept. At first a special group payment scheme was introduced: previously the girls had been grouped with one hundred other operatives for incentive payment purposes. Other changes introduced at various times were rest pauses in several different forms (varying in length and spacing), shorter hours and refreshments, in all more than ten changes. Before putting the changes into effect, the investigators spent a lot of time discussing them with the girls. Communication between the workers and the research team was very full and open throughout the experimental period. Almost without exception output increased with each change made.

The next stage in the experiment was to return to the original conditions. The operatives reverted to a forty-eight-hour six-day week, no incentives, no rest pauses and no refreshment. Output went up to the highest yet recorded. By this time it had become clear, to quote Mayo, 'that the itemized changes experimentally imposed . . . could not be used to explain the major change – the continually increasing production'. The explanation eventually given was that the girls experienced a tremendous increase in work satisfaction because they had greater freedom in their working environment and control over their own pace-setting. The six operatives had become a social group with their own standards and expectations. By removing the girls from the normal setting of work and by intensifying their interaction and cooperation, informal practices, values, norms and social relationships had been built up giving the group high cohesion. Also, the communication system between the researchers and the workers was extremely effective; this meant that the norms of output were those that the girls felt the researchers desired. The supervisors took a personal interest in each girl and showed pride in the record of the group. The result was that the workers and the supervisors developed a sense of participation and as a result established a completely new working pattern. Mayo's generalization was that work satisfaction depends to a large extent on the informal social pattern of the work group. Where norms of cooperativeness and high output are established because of a feeling of importance, physical conditions have little impact.

However, this is the explanation arrived at in later years. At the time of the actual experiment, the continually increasing output was regarded as something of a mystery so an inquiry was instituted into conditions in the factory at large. This took the form of an interview programme. It was quickly realized that such a programme told the researchers little about the actual conditions in the factory but a great deal about the attitudes of various employees. The major finding of this stage of the inquiry was that many problems of worker–management cooperation were the results of the emotionally based attitudes of the workers rather than of objective difficulties in the situation. Workers, thought Mayo, were activated by a 'logic of sentiment', whereas management is concerned with the 'logic of cost and efficiency'. Conflict is inevitable unless this difference is understood and provided for.

The third stage of the investigation was to observe a group performing a task in a natural setting, i.e. a non-experimental situation. A number of employees in what became known as the Bank Wiring Observation Room were under constant observation and their output recorded. It was found that they restricted their output; the group had a standard for output and this was not exceeded by any individual. The attitude of the members of the group towards the company's financial incentive scheme was one of indifference. The group was highly integrated with its own social structure and code of behaviour which clashed with that of management. Essentially this code was composed of solidarity on the part of the group against management. Not too much work should be done, that would be ratebusting; on the other hand, not too little work should be done, that would be chiselling. There was little recognition of the organization's formal allocation of roles. This was confirmation of the importance of informal social groupings in determining levels of output.

Taken as a whole, the significance of the Hawthorne investigation was in 'discovering' the informal organization which, it is now realized, exists in all organizations. It demonstrated the importance to individuals of stable social relationships in the work situation. It confirmed Mayo in his wider thinking that what he calls the 'rabble hypothesis' about human behaviour (that each individual pursues his own rational self-interest) was completely false. It confirmed his view that the breakdown of traditional values in society could be countered by creating a situation in industry conducive to spontaneous cooperation. For Mayo, one of the major tasks of management is to organize spontaneous cooperation, thereby preventing the further breakdown of society. As traditional attachments to community and family disappear, and as the workplace increases in importance, the support given by traditional institutions must now be given by the organization. Conflict, competition and disagreement between individuals are to be avoided by management understanding its role as providing the basis for group affiliation. From the end of the Hawthorne project to his death Mayo was interested in discovering how spontaneous cooperation could be achieved. It is this which has been the basis of the Human Relations movement, the use of the insights of the social sciences to secure the commitment of individuals to the ends and activities of the organization.

The impact of Hawthorne and Mayo on both management and academics has been tremendous. It led to a fuller realization and understanding of the 'human factor' in work situations. Central to this was the 'discovery' of the informal group as an outlet for the aspirations of the worker. His work also led to an emphasis on the importance of an adequate communication system, particularly upwards from workers to management. The investigation showed, to quote Mayo, that 'management succeeds or fails in proportion as it is accepted without reservation by the group as authority and leader'.

Bibliography

Mayo, E., *The Human Problems of an Industrial Civilization,* Macmillan, 1933.
Mayo, E., *The Social Problems of an Industrial Civilization,* Boston: Harvard University Graduate School of Business Administration, 1949.
Roethlisberger, F. J., and Dickson, W. J., *Management and the Worker,* Harvard University Press, 1949.

Rensis Likert and Douglas McGregor

Rensis Likert (1903–1981) was an American social psychologist who in 1949 established the Institute of Social Research at the University of Michigan. Until his retirement in 1969, he was thus at the head of one of the major institutions conducting research into human behaviour in organizations. On his retirement he formed Rensis Likert Associates, a consulting firm, to put his ideas about the management of organizations into wider practice. His books are based on the numerous research studies which he and his colleagues have conducted. His last book was jointly written with his research collaborator and wife, Jane Gibson Likert.

Douglas McGregor (1906–1964) was a social psychologist who published a number of research papers in this field. For some years he was President (i.e. Chief Executive) of Antioch College and he has described how this period as a top administrator affected his views on organizational functioning. From 1954 until his death, he was Professor of Management at the Massachusetts Institute of Technology.

'Managers with the best records of performance in American business and government are in the process of pointing the way to an appreciably more effective system of management than now exists,' proclaims Likert. Research studies have shown that departments which are low in efficiency tend to be in the charge of supervisors who are 'job-centred'. That is they 'tend to concentrate on keeping their subordinates busily engaged in going through a specified work cycle in a prescribed way and at a satisfactory rate as determined by time standards'. This attitude is clearly derived from that of Taylor (see p. 133) with its emphasis on breaking down the job into component parts, selecting and training people to do them, and exerting constant pressure to achieve output. The supervisor sees himself as getting the job done with the resources (which includes the people) at his disposal.

Supervisors with the best record of performance are found to focus their attention on the human aspects of their subordinates' problems, and on building effective work groups which are set high achievement goals. These supervisors are 'employee-centred'. They regard their jobs as dealing with human beings rather than with the work; they attempt to know them as individuals. They see their function as helping them to do the job efficiently. They exercise general rather than detailed supervision, and are more concerned with targets than methods. They allow maximum participation in decision-making. If high performance is to be obtained, a supervisor must not only be employee-centred but must also have high performance goals and be capable of exercising the decision-making processes to achieve them.

In summarizing these findings, Likert distinguishes four systems of management. System 1 is the exploitive authoritative type where management uses fear and threats, communication is downward, superiors and subordinates are psychologically far apart, the bulk of decisions is taken at the top of the organization, etc. System 2 is the benevolent authoritative type where management uses rewards, attitudes are subservient to superiors, information flowing upward is restricted to what the boss wants to hear, policy decisions are taken at the top but decisions within a prescribed framework may be delegated to lower levels, etc. System 3 is the consultative type where management uses rewards, occasional punishments and some involvement is sought, communication is both down and up but upward communication other than that which the boss wants to hear is given in limited amounts and only cautiously, although subordinates can have a moderate amount of influence on the activities of their departments as broad policy decisions are taken at the top and more specific decisions at lower levels, etc.

System 4 is characterized by participative group management. Management give economic rewards and make full use of group participation and involvement in setting high performance goals, improving work methods, etc.; communication flows downwards, upwards and with peers and is accurate; subordinates and superiors are very close psychologically. Decision-making is widely done throughout the organization through group processes, and is integrated into the formal structure by regarding the organization chart as a series of overlapping groups with each group linked to the rest of the organization by means of persons (called 'linking pins') who are members of more than one group. System 4 management produces high productivity, greater involvement of individuals, and better labour–management relations.

In general, high-producing managers are those who have built the personnel in their units into effective groups, whose members have cooperative attitudes and a high level of job satisfaction through System 4 management. But there are exceptions. Technically comp-etent, job-centred, tough management can achieve high productivity (particularly if backed up by tight systems of control techniques). But the members of units whose supervisors use these high-pressure methods are likely to have unfavourable attitudes towards their work and the management, and to have excessively high levels of waste and scrap. They also show higher labour turnover, and greater labour–management conflict as measured by work-stoppages, official grievances and the like.

Management, according to Likert, is always a relative process. To be effective and to communicate, a leader must always adapt his behaviour to take account of the *persons* whom he leads. There are no specific rules which will work well in all situations, but only general principles which must be interpreted to take account of the expectations, values and skills of those with whom the manager interacts. Sensitivity to these values and expectations is a crucial leadership skill, and organizations must create the atmosphere and conditions which encourage every manager to deal with the people he encounters in a manner fitting to their values and their expecta-tions.

To assist in this task, management now has available a number of measures of relevant factors which have been developed by social scientists. Methods are available to obtain objective measurements of such variables as: the amount of member loyalty to an organiza-tion; the extent to which the goals of groups and individuals facilitate the achievement of the organization's goals; the level of motivation among members; the degree of confidence and trust between different hierarchical levels and between different sub-units; the efficiency and adequacy of the communication process; the extent to which each superior is correctly informed of the expectations, reactions, obstacles, problems and failures of his sub-ordinates – together with the assistance they find useful and the assurance they wish they could get.

These measures and others enable an organization to know at any time the state of the system of functioning human beings which underpins it (called the 'interaction-influence system'); whether it is improving or deteriorating and why, and what to do to bring about desired improvements. This objective information about the interaction-influence system enables problems of leadership and management to be depersonalized and the 'authority of facts' to come to the fore. A much wider range of human behaviour can now be measured and made objective, whereas previously impressions and judgements had to suffice.

Douglas McGregor examines the assumptions about human behaviour which underlie managerial action. The traditional conception of administration (as exemplified by the writings of Fayol, pp. 63–7) is based upon the direction and control by management of the enterprise and its individual members. It implies certain basic assumptions about human motivation, which McGregor characterizes as 'Theory X'. These are:

1. 'The average human being has an inherent dislike of work and will avoid it if he can.' Thus management needs to stress productivity, incentive schemes and 'a fair day's work'; and to denounce 'restriction of output'.
2. 'Because of this human characteristic of dislike of work, most people must be coerced, controlled, directed, threatened with punishment to get them to put forth adequate effort toward the achievement of organizational objectives.'
3. 'The average human being prefers to be directed, wishes to avoid responsibility, has relatively little ambition, wants security above all.'

Theory X has persisted for a long time (although it is not usually stated as baldly as this). It has done so because it has undoubtedly provided an explanation for *some* human behaviour in organizations. There are, however, many readily observable facts and a growing body of research findings (such as those described by Likert) which cannot be explained on these assumptions. McGregor proposes an alternative 'Theory Y', with the underlying principle of 'integration' to replace direction and control. The assumptions about human motivation of Theory Y are:

1. 'The expenditure of physical and mental effort in work is as natural as play or rest.' The ordinary person does not inherently

dislike work: according to the conditions it may be a source of satisfaction or punishment.

2. External control is not the only means for obtaining effort. 'Man will exercise self-direction and self-control in the service of objectives to which he is committed.'

3. The most significant reward that can be offered in order to obtain commitment is the satisfaction of the individual's self-actualizing needs (compare Argyris, see p. 177). This can be a direct product of effort directed towards organizational objectives.

4. 'The average human being learns, under proper conditions, not only to accept but to seek responsibility.'

5. Many more people are able to contribute creatively to the solution of organizational problems than do so.

6. At present the potentialities of the average person are not being fully used.

McGregor develops an analysis of how the acceptance of Theory Y as the basis for running organizations would work out. He is particularly concerned with effects on performance appraisals, salaries and promotions, participation and staff–line relationships. On this last topic he makes the important point that there will be tension and conflict between staff and line as long as the staff departments are used as a service to top management to *control* the line (which is required by Theory X). With Theory Y the role of the staff is regarded as that of providing professional help to *all levels* of management.

The essential concept which both Likert and McGregor are propounding is that modern organizations, to be effective, must regard themselves as interacting groups of people with '*supportive relationships*' to each other. In the ideal, each member of the organization will feel that its objectives are of significance to him, that his job is meaningful, indispensable and difficult, that to do it effectively he needs and obtains support from his superiors – who regard the giving of this support to make *him* effective as their prime function.

In later work Likert and Likert extend the System 1 to 4 classification by identifying the 'System 4 Total Model Organization' (System 4T). This designation refers to organizations which have a number of characteristics in addition to those of System 4. These include: high levels of performance goals held by the leader and transmitted to subordinates, high levels of knowledge and skill of the leader with regard to technical issues, administration and problem-solving; the capacity of the leader to provide planning, resources equipment, training and help to subordinates. System 4T is also characterized by an optimum structure in terms of differentiation and linkages, and stable group working relationships.

System 4T is currently the best method for dealing with conflict because of its approach of getting appropriate data related to *group* needs (thus removing person-to-person conflict) and engaging in group decision-making in order to resolve the differences in the best interests of the entire organization. If members of one or both of the two groups shows an inability to use group decision-making techniques sufficiently well, then higher levels must provide further training in group processes. The interaction-influence system will develop a capacity for self-correction, since groups recognize those groups which are not performing their linking-pin and problem-solving functions effectively and can arrange for coaching and training. Correction is possible because the failures are picked up not by after-the-fact data (e.g. falling production, rising costs, lower earnings) but through the interaction-influence system, in the early stages before poor performance and conflict arise.

Likert's argument is that the nearer to System 4T the organization approaches the more productivity and profits will improve and conflict be reduced. Likert also suggests a System 5 organization of the future in which the authority of hierarchy will completely disappear. The authority of individuals will derive only from their linking-pin roles and from the influence exerted by the overlapping groups of which they are members.

Bibliography

Likert, R., *New Patterns of Management,* McGraw-Hill, 1961.
Likert, R., *The Human Organization: Its Management and Value,* McGraw-Hill, 1967.
McGregor, D., *The Human Side of Enterprise,* McGraw-Hill, 1960.
McGregor, D., *Leadership and Motivation,* MIT Press, 1966.
McGregor, D., *The Professional Manager,* McGraw-Hill, 1967.
Likert, R., and Likert, J. G., *New Ways of Managing Conflict,* McGraw-Hill, 1976.

Robert R. Blake and Jane S. Mouton

Robert Blake and Jane Mouton are respectively President and Vice-President of Scientific Methods, Inc., an organization which provides behavioural science consultancy services to industry. Both are psychologists, trained in American universities. Blake first designed and tested the 'Managerial Grid' during his subsequent employment in industry.

Blake and Mouton start from the assumption that a manager's job is to foster attitudes and behaviour which promote efficient performance, stimulate and use creativity, generate enthusiasm for experimentation and innovation, and learn from interaction with others. Such managerial competence can be taught and it can be learned. Their managerial grid provides a framework for understanding and applying effective management.

The grid sets the guidelines for an approach to management which has been widely applied. It has been successful in North America, in Europe, and in Asia; in production work, sales, and R & D, in trade unions, and in military, government, and welfare organizations. Its relevance appears to transcend cultural boundaries and forms of organization. Moreover, it has been applied from supervisory jobs to executive levels.

The managerial grid results from combining two fundamental ingredients of managerial behaviour. One is concern for production: the other is concern for people. 'Concern for' does not mean a dedication to specific targets, nor does it mean the results achieved in themselves. It means the general approach to management which governs the actions of a supervisor or manager, just *how* he concerns himself with production and with people.

Concern for production does not mean only physical factory products. The term 'production' can refer to the number of good research ideas, the number of accounts processed, the volume of sales, the quality of service given or of top policy decisions made, and so on. Concern for people similarly includes all of concern for friendships, for personal commitment to tasks, for someone's self-respect, for equitable payment, and so on.

Any manager's approach to management will show more or less of each of these two fundamental constituents. A manager may show a high degree of production concern together with low people concern, or the other way around. Or he may be middling on both. Indeed all of these are commonplace and it is also commonplace that none of these is satisfactory. Placing the two fundamentals as the axes of a graph enables a grid to be drawn which reveals very simply not only many typical combinations seen in the behaviour of managers every day, but also the desirable combination of 'concern for' as follows:

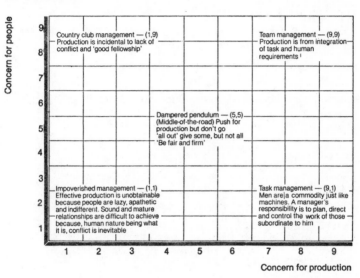

The Managerial Grid
(from Blake and Mouton, 'The managerial grid', *Advanced Management Office Executive*, 1962, vol. 1, no. 9)

Different positions on the grid represent different typical patterns of behaviour. The grid suggests that change could be towards *both* high concern for people (scores 9) and high concern for production (also scores 9) simultaneously, that is to a 9,9 managerial style of 'team management'.

The grid indicates that all degrees of concern for production and concern for people are possible; but for simplicity five styles of management are picked out for illustration.

9,1 management, or 'task management', focuses overwhelmingly on production. A 9,1 manager is an exacting taskmaster who expects schedules to be met and people to do what they are told, no more and no less. Anything that goes wrong will be viewed as due to someone's mistake, and that someone must be found and the blame squarely placed. Supervisors make decisions. Subordinates carry them out. The manager should run his own show, and disagreement is likely to be viewed as the next thing to insubordination. 9,1 management can achieve high production, at least in the short run, but it has a number of deficiencies. Any creative energies of subordinates go into how to defeat the system rather than how to improve it. Disagreements are ruled out and suppressed rather than settled. Subordinates do what is required, but no more, and seem 'obviously' indifferent and apathetic. Win–lose thinking is eventually reflected in the development of trade unions and struggles between unions and managements. 9,1 management is prevalent in a competitive industrial society such as the USA because inadequate education leaves many people unable to use more than limited skills and compelled to endure this kind of supervision.

The 1,9 managerial style, or 'country club management' as it has been called, emphasizes solely concern for people. It does not push people for production because 'you can lead a horse to water, but you can't make him drink'. People are encouraged and supported, and their mistakes are overlooked because they are doing the best they can. The key word is togetherness (as W. H. Whyte, p. 215) and informal conversation, coffee together, and a joke help things along. The informal rule is 'no work discussions during breaks'. But country club management also has deficiencies. People try to avoid direct disagreements or criticisms of one another and production problems are glossed over. No one should be upset even if work is not going quite as it should. New ideas which might cause trouble or objectives which would cause strain are let slide. The 1,9 style easily grows up in quasi-monopoly situations or when operating on a cost-plus basis, and its ultimate end may be the complete closing of a non-competitive unit.

Little concern for either production or people results in 'impoverished management', the 1,1 style. It is difficult to imagine a whole organization surviving for long with this kind of management, but it is frequent enough in individual managers and supervisors. 1,1 management is characterized by the avoidance of responsibility or personal commitment. The supervisor leaves people to work as they think fit. He does just enough so that if anything goes wrong he can say 'I told them what to do – it's not my problem.' He minimizes contacts with anyone and is noncommittal on any problems which come to him. The 1,1 approach typically reveals the frustration of someone who has been passed over for promotion, shunted sideways, or has been for years in a routine job (as Argyris, p. 178, also suggests).

Managers frequently alternate between the 1,9 'country club' style and the 9,1 'task management' style. They tighten up to increase output, 9,1 style, but when human relationships begin to suffer the pendulum swings right across to 1,9 again. The middle of the managerial grid shows the 5,5 'dampened pendulum' style, typified by marginal shifts around the happy medium. This middle-of-the-road style pushes enough to get acceptable production but yields enough to maintain acceptable morale. To aim fully for both is too idealistic. The manager aims at a moderate carrot-and-stick standard, fair but firm, and has confidence in his subordinate's ability to meet targets. 5,5 management thus gives rise to 'splitting the difference' on problems, to attempting balanced solutions rather than appropriate ones.

Unlike 5,5 management, and all the other styles, 9,9 'team management' shows high concern for production and high concern for people, and does not accept that these concerns are incompatible. The team manager seeks to integrate people around production. Morale is task-related. Unlike 5,5, the 9,9 style tries to discover the best and most effective solutions, and aims at the highest attainable production to which all involved contribute and in which everyone finds his own sense of accomplishment. People satisfy their own needs through the job and working with others, not through incidental sociability in the 'country club' style. The 9,9 manager assumes that employees who know what the stakes are for them and others in what they are doing will not need boss direction and control (as Likert, p. 164). The manager's responsibility is to see to it that work is planned and organized by those with a stake in it and not necessarily by himself. Objectives should be clear to all, and though demanding should be realistic. It is accepted that conflict will occur, but problems are confronted directly and openly and not as personal disputes. This encourages creativity. Sustained improvement of the form of organization and development of those in it are both aims and likely outcomes of a 9,9 style.

Blake and Mouton reject most strongly a contingency approach to leadership and decision-making (see Fiedler, p. 187, and Vroom, p. 119). Contingency theorists argue that particular leadership styles are appropriate to particular situations. This is to say that there are certain circumstances where a 9,1 or a 1,9 style would be the most appropriate. Blake and Mouton dispute this very static approach for it does not appear to consider the adverse longer-term effects of, for example, a 9,1 style in the negative consequences for the leader's health and career and the lack of growth or stunting of subordinates.

The 9,9 leadership style is always the best since it builds on long-term development and trust. A leader whose subordinates expect or want 9,1 or 1,9 leadership should train them so that they can understand and respond to 9,9. In this way their own development will be improved. The 9,9 approach should be adopted with versatility but the principles should be firmly retained.

9,9 management implicitly assumes a certain approach to conflict, both individual and between groups such as departments, headquarters office and field staff, labour and management, or the managements of newly merged corporations. In their book, *Managing Intergroup Conflict*, Blake and Mouton together with Herbert Shepherd examine common reactions to such conflict and again suggest a style or approach which may lead to better solutions.

Many managers assume that conflicts are inevitable and cannot be resolved as such. If A and B disagree, then the result must favour one or the other. There may be a win–lose power struggle; or reference to a third party (e.g. overall boss) for a decision; or a stalemate which leaves the conflict unresolved until something happens which settles it or removes it, i.e. 'fate arbitration'. A second kind of assumption is that conflict can be avoided since groups need not be interdependent and can get on with things separately. Under this approach, one party to a disagreement gives up and withdraws; or both parties isolate themselves from the other; or everyone concerned puts on a façade of indifference. Third,

2. The performance of the leader depends as much on situational favourableness as it does on the style of the person in the leadership position. The crucial factor is that the style of the leader and the work group situation should be matched. This *leader match* and its appropriate benefits can be obtained either by trying to change the leader's style or by trying to change the situation in which he operates.

Fiedler has consistently maintained that the first of the change options to achieve leader match (changing the leader's style) is unrealistic and that leadership training which attempts to do this (e.g. to increase openness or employee-centredness) has not been effective because the leadership-style motivational pattern is too stable a characteristic of the individual (see Vroom, p. 123, for an opposing view). From Fiedler's point of view, what appropriate training does – together with experience – is to give the leader more technical knowledge and administrative know-how to enable him to increase his influence and control and thus to get into a more favourable situation. But the contingency approach indicates that in many of the octants a more favourable situation (e.g. moving from Octant 8 to Octant 4 by improving leader–member relations) requires a different leadership style. Hence while training and experience will improve the performance of one type of leader whose new octant situation would now be matched to his style, it will *decrease* the performance of the other style type who has lost his matching. Training therefore must be undertaken with knowledge of leadership style in relation to the leader's situation, otherwise on average it is bound to have no effect.

Changing the situation in which the leader operates to one which calls for his leadership style is a more appropriate way of achieving the leader match. Thus we might increase the favourableness of a task-motivated leader's situation to one which made a better match by giving him more explicit instructions to work to, and more authority to achieve the tasks (Octant 4 to Octant 1). *Decreasing* the favourableness of the situation in order to improve the leader's performance by a better match is not as unusual as it first might appear. Managers are frequently transferred to more 'challenging' jobs because they have become bored or stale. 'Challenging' could well mean that there are awkward people to work with and the authority is much diminished – but a move of a relationship-motivated leader from Octant 1 to Octant 6 would improve the match and his performance.

Thus successful organizations are those which give each leader a good evaluation of his own and his group's performance and which make him aware of the situations under which he performs best. The good leader will develop situations in which his leadership style is most likely to succeed.

Bibliography

Fiedler, F. E., 'Engineer the job to fit the manager', *Harvard Business Review* 43 (1965), 115-22.

Fiedler, F. E., *A Theory of Leadership Effectiveness,* McGraw-Hill, 1967.

Fiedler, F. E., 'How do you make leaders more effective? New answers to an old puzzle', *Organization Dynamics* I (1972) 3-18.

Fiedler, F. E., Chemers, M. M., and Mahar, L., *Improving Leadership Effectiveness: the Leader Match Concept* (rev. edn), Wiley, 1977.

Elliott Jaques and
the Glacier Investigations

Elliott Jaques is a Canadian who graduated in psychology at the University of Toronto and later in medicine at the Johns Hopkins Medical School. After service in the Royal Canadian Army Medical Corps, he joined the staff of the Tavistock Institute of Human Relations, where over a period of years he led a study of worker and management activities in the Glacier Metal Company – an engineering factory in London whose managing director was Wilfred Brown, himself a well-known writer on management issues. The Glacier Investigations may well come to bear comparison with the Hawthorne Studies for their impact on management thinking. For this work Jaques was awarded a Doctorate of Philosophy in the Department of Social Relations at Harvard University. He is a qualified psychoanalyst and has worked as a psychotherapist and as a 'social therapist' to the Glacier Company. Since 1965, Jaques has been Professor of Social Science and Director of the Institute of Organization and Social Studies at Brunel University, where he has worked with the National Health Service, the Church of England, and with many commercial and public organizations in Europe and America.

Jaques and his collaborators in the Glacier Investigations use the technique of 'action research'. They work in collaboration with members of the firm to study psychological and social forces affecting group behaviour; to develop more effective ways of resolving social stress; and to facilitate agreed and desired social change.

The problems they tackle are those on which particular groups in the organization request their help. Thus Jaques's book *The Changing Culture of a Factory* describes, for example, studies of problems of payment and morale in the Service Department, worker–management cooperation in the Works Committee, executive leadership at the Divisional Managers' meeting. The method used consists of the 'working-through' (by the investigator and the group together) of current problems and their possible solutions. The investigator attends meetings of the group, and interprets to it the social and personal factors at play in an attempt to increase the social and psychological insight of the group. This also promotes a more rational attitude to social change.

The 'working-through' process usually leads to the discovery that the apparent problems of the group are only symptoms of more basic and long-term difficulties and these are then examined. What began as an issue of wages and methods of payment in the Service Department, for example, soon developed into the complex ramifications of inter-group stresses so often associated with wage questions. As a result of the working-through of management and worker differences at a series of meetings of representatives of both sides (which was facilitated by the investigator's interpretations), not only was the change-over to a new system of payment accomplished, but in the new situation created by these discussions it was possible to institute a Shop Council as a continuing mechanism through which members could take part in setting policy for the department.

One of the most important findings to come out of the Glacier Investigations is the individual's felt need to have his role and status clearly defined in a way which is acceptable both to himself and to his colleagues. Where there is some confusion of role boundaries, or where multiple roles occupied by the same person are not sufficiently distinguished, insecurity and frustration result. The study of the Divisional Managers' meeting showed that it functioned sometimes as an executive management committee taking decisions for the London factory, sometimes as a group for non-decision-making discussions with the Managing Director, and sometimes as a concealed Board of Directors for the whole company (including the Scottish factory). In this mixture of different functions, the same group had different powers over the affairs of the organization, depending on the particular capacity in which it was functioning. But these powers were not clear and this was personally disturbing to the members.

Even when a role has been defined it may contain elements which the individual finds unacceptable or difficult to fill. In an organization committed to consultative management, a superior may become increasingly unwilling to exercise his authority. Jaques describes some mechanisms by which he may avoid responsibility and authority. One is the exercise of a consultative relationship only. Thus the Managing Director failed to perceive that he also held a role as chief executive of the London factory, and adopted only a consultative Managing Director's role to the Divisional Managers. This left a gap in the executive hierarchy. Another mechanism is the misuse of the process of formal joint consultation. This often provides an escape route from accepting responsibility for immediate subordinates, by making possible easy and direct contact between higher management and workers' representatives. Thus to make consultative management work, the consultation must follow the chain of command; otherwise conflict arises from those by-passed. Yet another evasive possibility is pseudo-democracy: a superior asserting 'I'm just an ordinary member of this committee' when he is in fact the senior person present; or a superior avoiding the leadership role by excessive delegation. One of the most important conclusions is that there is a distinctive leadership role in groups that members expect to be properly filled; and groups do not function well unless it is.

At the conclusion of these Tavistock studies, Jaques changed his position, becoming, with the consent of the workers' representatives, a part-time employee of the firm. He still retained his independent position, however, and continued his role as 'social analyst', working on problems of wages and salaries. Previous discussion had revealed continuous problems arising from supposed unfair differences in pay, and the task was to determine the appropriate payment and status of individuals. How can one establish what will be generally accepted as the right level of pay for a given job, particularly in relation to other jobs?

Work was divided by Jaques into its prescribed and its discretionary content. Prescribed work is specified in such a way as to leave nothing to the judgement of the individual doing it. But *all* jobs have some content, however small, which requires the individual to use discretion. From this developed the concept of the 'time-span of discretion' – the idea that the main criterion by which the importance of a job is implicitly evaluated is the length of time which expires before decisions taken by an individual are reviewed and evaluated. At the lowest level what the individual does is frequently checked, but at the highest level it might take several years before the effectiveness of a decision shows up. This approach is developed by Jaques in *The Measurement of Responsibility*.

Jaques finds that there is not a continuous increase in range of time-spans of discretion as one goes up the organization – in fact the changes go in steps. He identifies seven major strata (although there are sub-steps within each) up to three months, up to one year, two years, five years, ten years, twenty years, more than twenty years. These are generally recognized as clear differences of level, worthy of differences in payment. Those working in level one accept that those with level two discretion should be paid more and all would feel it inequitable if they were not. Differentials in 'felt-fair pay' – what people think they and others should earn – are very highly correlated (0.9 in the Glacier Metal Company) with objective measurements of differences in time-span, so that if a payment system is based on the discretion differences between jobs it will generally be seen as equitable.

A third element is the growth in capacity of the individual to operate with greater discretion, and Jaques presents earning progression curves which identify appropriate payments for those capable of, and on their way to, higher levels of discretion. An individual functions best when working at a level which corresponds to his capacity and for which he obtains equitable payment, and appropriate opportunity must be given for individuals to progress to their maximum time-span capacity.

These arguments are developed in *Free Enterprise, Fair Employment* to reject both Keynesian and Friedmanite economic measures as inadequate for dealing with self-perpetuating inflationary movements which then cause unemployment. Jaques argues that any nation has as much work as it wants for everyone, regardless of economic conditions. But there is one prime condition for full employment without inflation: the achievement of equitable pay differentials by political consensus based on the equitable work payment-scale appropriate to different time-span levels. Jaques presents evidence that in 1980, for example, the equitable annual wage and salary levels for a time-span of discretion of three months was £7,000 in England and $20,500 in the US, whereas for a two year time-span job it was £19,500 and $60,000. (The actual monetary levels will, of course, change over the years depending upon the rate of earnings inflation.)

The figures are not for the *actual* levels of pay in 1980 but for what people felt was differentially fair at that time. Any systematic policy for wages and salaries must decide (i) what the general level should be this year compared with last year, and (ii) whether any adjustment of differentials is called for – should the rates for the time-span levels be compressed, or expanded, in the whole of the range or part of the range, etc. These are the issues for a rational policy and Jaques maintains they would be accepted as just and fair as long as the differences in time-span of discretion were objectively determined and recognized.

Levels of time-span of discretion and the individual's work capacity to operate in these are also the keys to Jaques's general theory of bureaucracy. A bureaucracy in Jaques's terms is a hierarchically stratified employment system in which employees are accountable to their bosses for work that they do. This particular definition (which is somewhat different from the usual one – see Weber, p. 17) means that, for example, universities which have collegiate accountability of academic staff, or trade unions which have electoral accountability of full-time officers, are not bureaucracies in this sense. Jaques is insistent that neither his theory of bureaucracy nor his theories of time-span of discretion and equitable payment are intended to apply in such organizations.

In bureaucracies (such as business firms, government agencies, armed services) Jaques has found that ascending the hierarchy involves operating with increasing time-spans and that the basic seven strata of time-span correspond with levels of thinking capability from concrete thinking at the bottom end to abstract modelling and institution-creating at the top. The capacity to operate at longer time-spans with higher levels of abstraction in reasoning is the determinant of effectiveness at the higher levels of bureaucracy. The reason why bureaucracies are pyramidal in shape is that this work capacity (which Jaques maintains is innate) is very differentially distributed in human populations. Fewer are capable of the higher abstractions, and this is indeed generally recognized by organization members. It is this consensus which would allow equitable payment based on time-span capacity to operate economic competition *without* the exploitation of labour.

Bibliography

Jaques, E., *The Changing Culture of a Factory,* London: Tavistock, 1951.
Jaques, E., *The Measurement of Responsibility,* Tavistock, 1956.
Jaques, E., *Equitable Payment,* Wiley, 1961.
Jaques, E., *A General Theory of Bureaucracy,* Heinemann, 1976.
Jaques, E., *Free Enterprise, Fair Employment,* New York: Crane Russak, 1982.
Brown, W., and Jaques, E., *Glacier Project Papers,* Exeter, NH: Heinemann, 1965.

Edward E. Lawler III

Edward E. Lawler is Professor of Organizational Behavior and Director of the Center for Effective Organizations at the University of Southern California. An organizational psychologist, he has been concerned with a range of programmes of research and action research into management effectiveness, quality of working life and innovative approaches to designing and managing organizations. His continuing interest in the psychological analysis of the part that pay and reward systems play in organizational effectiveness and organizational change led, in 1972, to his receiving a Distinguished Scientific Award from the American Compensation Association.

Lawler's interest in appropriate systems for pay and reward stems from his view, based on a considerable amount of research both of his own and of others, that compensation has an important influence on those behaviours which lead to organizational effectiveness. In a recent survey of research studies, four methods used to improve productivity were compared. Incentive payments yielded the highest average increase (30 per cent); goal-setting, e.g. management by objectives (see Drucker, p. 143) and job enrichment (see Herzberg, p. 184), each had under 20 per cent, and participation only one half per cent. Thus, argues Lawler, any change to be effective (including participation) should be linked to appropriate changes in payment systems.

This is because pay is so important to the individual in the organization. It not only enables him to satisfy his material needs and gives a feeling of security, but also, very important for many people, pay is seen as a mark of the esteem in which they are held, as well as providing opportunities to engage in activities which are autonomously directed and independent of the work organization.

Why then, in spite of its importance both to organizations as a determinant of effectiveness and to individuals as a source of satisfaction, is pay so often an organizational problem? Studies have shown that in many organizations 50 per cent or more of employees are dissatisfied with their pay. In a major US sample survey, the percentage of people who agreed that they received 'good' pay and fringe benefits dropped from 48 per cent to 34 per cent between 1973 and 1977.

There are a number of conclusions from research which can explain this situation. Satisfaction with pay is a function of how much is received compared with how much the individual feels should be received. Ideas of what should be received are based on two factors.

The first factor is an evaluation of what contribution the individual makes in terms of his skill, experience, age, amount of responsibility, etc. Typically individuals rate their personal contributions higher than other people rate them. (Surveys have shown that the average employee rates his performance in the top 20 per cent of his grade!) They also consider that the contributions in which they are strong (e.g. formal education, company loyalty) should be weighted most heavily, and those in which they are weak (e.g. seniority on the job, difficulty of task) should be regarded as less important.

The second factor contributing to ideas of appropriate payment is a comparison of what happens to other similar people both within and outside the organization. Often there is a lack of correct information about the rewards of others, because this is an emotional issue and organizations keep the results of salary surveys, performance appraisals and individual remuneration secret. On the whole, therefore, people tend to overestimate the pay of others doing similar work.

Not surprisingly, then, there is dissatisfaction with rewards and this leads to reduced motivation, absenteeism, labour turnover, and difficulties in recruitment. What can be done to attack these problems? Since dissatisfaction stems from relativities and comparisons, paying everybody more money will clearly not improve the situation. Lawler maintains that it is possible *within the same total wage bill* to redesign the payment and benefit system to obtain increased individual satisfaction and organizational effectiveness.

There are a number of major organizational characteristics which influence what would be the nature of an appropriate compensation plan for a particular enterprise:

1. *Organizational climate.* Using the distinction made by Likert and McGregor (p. 164) it is clear an organization with a participative climate (System 4, Theory Y) can use participative methods for disclosure of information, setting of objectives, generation of trust to allow changes, etc. In such an organization it might be agreed, for example, that an all-salary payment system is appropriate because there is sufficient trust and confidence in supervision that unfair advantage will not be taken by anyone through slacking, absenteeism, etc. An authoritarian climate on the other hand (System 1, Theory X) would do well to emphasize 'hard' criteria, e.g. quantity of output and sales, since these can be monitored in detail and thus require a much lower level of trust and openness.

2. *Technology.* The distinctions of Woodward (p. 26) of unit, mass and process production will affect the payment system. Individual performance measures may be appropriate in unit and mass, but plant-wide measures are necessary for process industry. In non-industrial professional service organizations (e.g. hospitals, schools) attempts to tie rewards to control measures of performance would be likely to result in increased bureaucratic behaviour. Joint goal-setting would be more appropriate here.

3. *Size and organization structure.* The size of an organization will affect the possibilities; small enterprises can use company-wide indices of performance thus emphasizing the common endeavour. For large organizations this is inevitably seen as irrelevant by an individual employee (unless he is right at the top). Decentralized organizations can link payment schemes to the performance of the sub-unit, but there must be real delegation of decision-making power to the sub-unit (e.g. factory) to affect its own performance, otherwise effort will be directed to defeating the control system, not to improving effectiveness.

The pay system must therefore fit the characteristics of an organization if it is to be effective. Appropriate merit pay plans for different types of organization are presented in the table.

Appropriate merit pay plans for various types of organizations

Organization	Type	Size	Centralization	Plan
Authoritarian	Mass and unit	Large	Cent.	Individual basis; objective criteria
			Decent.	For workers – individual; for managers – group plan possible on profit centre basis; for all objective criteria
		Small	Cent.	Individual basis; objective criteria
			Decent.	For workers – individual; for managers – group plan possible on profit centre basis; for all objective criteria
	Process	Large	Cent.	None very appropriate; companywide bonus possible for managers
			Decent.	Group plan based upon objective sub-unit performance criteria
		Small	Cent.	Organizationwide bonus plan
			Decent.	Group plan based upon objective sub-unit performance measures
	Professional service	Large	Cent.	None appropriate
			Decent.	None appropriate
		Small	Cent.	None appropriate
			Decent.	None appropriate
Democratic	Mass and unit	Large	Cent.	Individual plans based on objective criteria as well as soft criteria, such as participatively set goals
			Decent.	Same as centralized, but for managers use data from their sub-part of organization
		Small	Cent.	Some consideration to performance of total organization; individual plans based on objective criteria as well as soft criteria, such as participatively set goals
			Decent.	Same as centralized except sub-part performance can be used as criteria in both individual and group plans
	Process	Large	Cent.	Organizationwide plan based on objective and subjective criteria; individual appraisal based on soft criteria
			Decent.	Group plan based on plant performance, objective and subjective criteria
		Small	Cent.	Organizationwide plan based on company performance
			Decent.	Group plans based on sub-unit performance
	Professional	Large	Cent.	Design individual plans; high input from employees; joint goal setting and evaluation
			Decent.	Same as centralized but some consideration to performance of sub-parts
		Small	Cent.	Some consideration to performance of total organization; design individual plans; high input from employees; joint goal setting and evaluation
			Decent.	Same as centralized, except that data for sub-part of organization may be relevant

from Lawler (1971)

The characteristics of the organization and the characteristics of the pay system must be matched, but there are two ways in which this can be done. We can choose the correct system for the present organizational characteristics or we can change the organization to fit the plan. Because pay is so important to individuals, is so tangible in its effects and has system-wide implications, simultaneously changing the pay system is crucial in ensuring that other changes are effective. For example, the continued administration of a traditional authoritarian pay system could well ensure that an avowed move to more participative management will be regarded as insincere and a management gimmick. An appropriate new pay system can signal to all that a real change is taking place.

There are many changes taking place in regard to work organizations which have implications for new payment systems. For example, the workforce is becoming more heterogeneous, multicultural, with greater participation of women and of minority groups in more senior positions. People are becoming more educated and knowledgeable, less accepting of traditional authority with an increasing desire for more influence at the workplace. The nature of organizations is changing (more service organizations and less manufacturing ones, large organizations are getting larger and more diversified, but large numbers of small businesses are coming into being and surviving) and so is the environment in which they operate. Slower economic growth, which seems likely for developed countries, together with all these other changes, will inevitably intensify people's concern with social equity and thus make it ever more imperative that payment systems should motivate performance and give individual satisfaction.

Lawler identifies a number of practices which are being introduced to deal with such changes. Of primary importance is the concept of *individualization of compensation systems*. Plans that use the same pay methods in all parts of the organization and give everybody the same benefits using the same basic rates, etc., no longer fit both the diverse workforce and the diverse nature of organizations. More individual contracts with greater flexibility on working hours, pay–performance relationships, balance between salary and fringe benefits and so on are needed. This is already done for managers at the top but will have to percolate further down the organizational levels to give people greater choice in meeting their reward requirements. Such traditional practices as the blanket distinction between hourly and salaried employees will more and more come into question.

Some further trends, which do not sit easily together, may also be noted. Performance-based pay systems (where they are appropriate) are becoming more important in linking pay to performance in a motivating way. But they must be carried out in the light of modern feelings that decisions about pay should be arrived at by open and defensible processes not by a secret personal top-down approach, lacking any appeal procedure. Also, more egalitarian reward systems, which decrease the number of grade levels and set limits to the differences in rewards, go in harness with the desire of many for more open participative organizations but may well relate less directly to performance.

There are no automatic answers to these issues. 'As society changes, so must its organizations; as organizations change, so must their pay systems.'

Bibliography

Lawler, E. E., *Pay and Organizational Effectiveness: A Psychological View,* McGraw-Hill, 1971.
Lawler, E. E., *Pay and Organization Development,* Addison-Wesley, 1981.

6 · *The Organization in Society*

Who says organization, says oligarchy.
Robert Michels

What is occurring ... is a drive for social dominance, for power and privilege, for the position of ruling class, by the social group or class of the manager.
James Burnham

We do need to know how to cooperate with the Organization but, more than ever, so do we need to know how to resist it.
William H. Whyte

The danger to liberty lies in the subordination of belief to the needs of the industrial system.
J. K. Galbraith

Small is beautiful.
Fritz Schumacher

Organizations do not exist or operate in a vacuum. They are one sort of institution in a particular society. They have to conform to the needs and standards laid down by institutions other than themselves. The pressures of a market economy, political decisions, legal restrictions, all affect organizational operations. Yet the large-scale organization is one of the dominant institutions of our time, and in its turn must exert a powerful influence on the rest of society. Many writers have taken up this theme and have tried to show how far the nature of modern organizations has changed society.

Robert Michels argues that modern large organizations inevitably produce a powerful oligarchy at the top with considerable social consequences. James Burnham examines how the balance of power in society has shifted from the owners of wealth to those who manage it. For William H. Whyte also, managers are an increasingly assertive section of society and he is alarmed that their characters are being moulded by the organization which employs them.

J. K. Galbraith underlines the inadequacy of the market mechanism for regulating economies, and points to the consequent frequent intervention of governments as a 'countervailing power'. Fritz Schumacher warns against believing that the problems of production have been solved when we are using up the resources of our planet at a rate which cannot continue.

Robert Michels

Robert Michels (1876–1936) was a German sociologist and political scientist, writing at the beginning of this century. Like many of those who were involved in the early development of ideas in the social sciences he was politically as well as scientifically committed. He was a socialist until, as he came to the end of his life, and as a result of his own theorizing, he turned towards the fascist ideas of Mussolini. His political life informed his social theories and his social theories influenced his political life.

What was it, then, that caused Michels to move from the left to the right of politics? His move derived from the contradiction that he perceived in the internal structure and functioning of organizations: the contradiction between democracy and bureaucracy. For Michels, the essential principle of organizational functioning is 'the iron law of oligarchy'. This 'iron law' means that whenever an organization is created it inevitably becomes controlled by a small group of people who use the organization to further their own interests rather than those of other organizational members. His main concern is to examine the organizational features which make internal democracy impossible and the displacement of objectives certain.

To understand how Michels arrived at his pessimistic view of organizational life it is necessary to put him in the context of his times and to examine the kinds of organizations he was primarily interested in. Those observing and writing about society during the latter half of the nineteenth century and the beginning of the twentieth saw the rise of the large-scale organization. Not only was it becoming apparent in industrial life, but also in politics and government. The extension of voting to more and more individuals led to political parties. The beginnings of the welfare state and increasing governmental activity meant the expansion of the civil service. Michels analyses the interaction between increasing organizational scale and the growth of bureaucracy.

His particular concern is with political parties and the state. The first mass-based political parties were appearing with the avowed aim of opening up politics, and consequently influence on the state, to a wider population than ever before. Political parties, and especially those of the left such as the German Social Democratic party, were democratic in structure. But for Michels the democracy of such parties quickly becomes a matter of formal structures, rule-books and constitutions; the actual functioning is something different – elite domination by means of a bureaucratic organization. The emergence of a bureaucratic elite is inevitable; it is 'the iron law of oligarchy'.

Michels suggests that as an organization gets bigger, so it becomes more bureaucratic. Political parties strive for larger membership. If they are successful and grow, they produce a larger hierarchy. They recruit full-time salaried officials and expert, professional leadership. There is a concentration of the means of communication, of information and of knowledge at the top of an organization. Because of its size and the bureaucratic mode of operation that this entails, a high level of participation is impossible in the large organization. A number of important consequences result.

Once an elite leadership and full-time officials have appeared there is the inevitability of a difference between the leaders and the led. This is particularly the case in voluntary organizations. The role of those at the top of an organization is to present the views and aspirations of the mass of members. But with the advent of specialized personnel and a dominant elite, the gap between the top and the bottom of an organization gets wider and wider. In these circumstances the leaders no longer represent the interests of the membership. So it is that an organization with a bureaucratic structure comes to be operated in the interests of its leaders who are concerned with the preservation of the bureaucracy. The leaders wish to maintain their positions because of the prestige and influence that go with that position. The salaried officials are self-interested because of the career possibilities that a well-developed bureaucracy offers. Together these consititute bureaucratic conservatism.

The processes of self-interest and bureaucratic conservatism together produce a slackening of the revolutionary ideas and fervour which Michels sees as necessary for a left-wing political organization. Indeed, such ideas become supplanted by ideologies which stress the need for internal unity, the need for harmony of views and ideas, and the undesirability of having conflicts and tensions in the organization. Stress is also placed on the hostility of the surrounding environment, the external enemies and the danger of exposing internal difficulties and differences. With a professional leadership that is cut off from the mass of members, the organization becomes an end in itself rather than a means towards non-organizational ends such as equality or democracy. Because of its scale and bureaucratic nature it serves the interests of the elite.

Although primarily concerned with the problem of internal democracy in political parties, Michels broadened his argument in two ways. First, he demonstrated the link between organizational and societal oligarchy. The leaders of organizations will be socially and culturally different from the led; indeed they will be members of the politically dominant classes, maintaining their positions through the control of organizations. In addition the expanding middle classes will be able to find security of employment through the growth of state organizations and thus enter into an alliance with the political elite as the servants of power (see Burnham, p. 211, for another view of the emergence of managerial powers).

Secondly, Michels maintains that 'the iron law of oligarchy' is applicable not just to political and voluntary organizations, but to all organizations subject to increasing scale, because of the inherent opposition of bureaucracy and democracy. Agreeing with Weber (p. 17), Michels sees the development of bureaucratic structures as an inevitable aspect of organizational growth. The processes of specialization and hierarchy which are the basis of bureaucracy are inimical to democracy because of their effects on decision-making and communication.

Michels sees no way out of his cycle of despair other than through periodic revolutionary and charismatic movements. Unfortunately (from his point of view) such movements rapidly become institutionalized and subject to the processes of oligarchy. For Michels the outlook for democracy was poor, and eventually his personal answer lay in a charismatic political movement – the fascism of Mussolini.

Michels gave the first expression to a problem that has concerned many writers since the turn of the century; namely, can large organizations retain democratic functioning, or will an inimical bureaucracy inevitably take over?

Bibliography

Michels, R., *Political Parties,* New York: Free Press, 1949. (First published in German in 1911)

James Burnham

James Burnham was born in 1905. He went to the University of Princeton and to Balliol College, Oxford, and from 1932 to 1954 was Professor of Philosophy at New York University. In 1955 he became editor of the *National Review*. During the thirties he was a member of the Trotskyite 'Fourth International', but he broke his Marxist connection in 1939. His many publications are mainly on political topics.

The term 'managerial revolution' has become part of the language since Burnham made it the title of his best-known book, written in 1940. As he himself points out, his views are not all that original, but they do constitute an attempt to formulate and argue logically about certain ideas which many people have wondered about, both then and since.

Burnham's thesis is that a declining capitalist form of society is giving way not to Marxist socialism, as is often suggested, but to a 'managerial society'. The managerial revolution by which this is being accomplished is not a violent upheaval but rather a transition over a period of time, in much the same way as feudal society gave way to capitalism. A wide range of symptoms heralded the imminent demise of capitalism as the Second World War commenced. The capitalist nations were unable to cope with mass unemployment, with permanent agricultural depression, and with the rapid rise in public and private debt. Their major ideologies of individualism, 'natural rights' of property, and private initiative were no longer accepted by the mass of the people.

But there is no reason to think that socialism is the inevitable consequence. Almost everywhere the Marxist parties are insignificant as a political force. The working class is declining in relative size and power. In Russia, the abolition of private property rights, which in Marxist theory should bring a classless socialist society, has neither prevented a ruling class from emerging nor promoted workers' control. Nevertheless, 'though Russia did not move toward socialism, at the same time it did not move back to capitalism'. What happened in Russia, as is steadily happening throughout the world, was a movement towards a managerial type of society. In this society it will be the managers who are dominant, who have power and privilege, who have control over the means of production, and have preference in the distribution of rewards. In short, the managers will be the ruling class. This does not necessarily mean that the political offices will be occupied by managers, any more than under capitalism all politicians were capitalists, but that the real power over what is done will be in the hands of managers.

In order to define who the managers are, Burnham singles out four groups of people with different functions. There are stock-holders, whose relationship to a company is entirely passive. There are financiers – capitalists whose interest is the financial aspects of numbers of companies irrespective of what those companies do. There are executives who guide a company, watch its profits and its prices. There are those who have charge of the technical process of producing, who organize men, materials and equipment, who develop the know-how which is becoming increasingly indispens-able. These last are the managers. Of the stockholders, financiers, executives and managers, only the managers are vital to the process of production. This has been demonstrated by state ownership in Russia, and by the extension of state enterprise in other nations. Moreover, even where private owners continue, they have been getting farther and farther away from the instruments of pro-duction, delegating supervision of production to others, exercising control at second, third or fourth hand through financial devices.

Burnham remarks on the self-confidence of managers compared with bankers, owners, workers, farmers and shopkeepers. These latter display doubts and worries, but managers have a self-assurance founded on the strength of their position. In managerial society there is no sharp distinction between politics and the arena of economics. In the state commissions, the committees, the bureaux, the administrative agencies, managers and bureaucrats coalesce. Rules, regulations and laws come increasingly to be issued by these interconnected bodies. The law is to be found in their records rather than in the annals of parliament. So in many nations sovereignty is gradually shifting from parliament to the admin-istrative offices.

In such an economy the managers will exercise power by occupying the key directing positions. But their preferential rewards will be less in wealth and property rights than in status in the political–economic structure.

Burnham also sees the outlines of the managerial ideologies which will replace the individualistic capitalist ideologies. The stress will be on the state, the people, the race; on planning rather than freedom, jobs rather than opportunity, duties and order rather than natural right.

Burnham's analysis of the overall trends in society and his projection of these into the future arouse interest to the extent that events bear him out. He was writing as the Second World War began. Much that has happened since could be construed, either way, for or against his arguments. Years later, W. H. Whyte's description of The Organization and Organization Man is in keeping with Burnham's forecast. Is there a managerial revolution?

Bibliography

Burnham, J., *The Managerial Revolution,* Peter Smith, 1941.

William H. Whyte

The American writer William H. Whyte is a journalist, and a student of the society in which he lives. He was born in 1917, and graduated in English at Princeton University in 1939. He has been on the staff of *Fortune* and has published articles in this and other leading magazines.

Whyte has concerned himself with contemporary trends in American society, and his book *The Organization Man* is an attempt to portray vividly one such trend which Whyte himself feels can go too far. He points to the coming of an organization man who not only works for The Organization but belongs to it as well. Such a man is a member of the middle class who occupy the middle rankings in all the great self-perpetuating institutions. Few of these ever become top managers, but they have 'taken the vows of organization life' and committed themselves to it.

Whyte argues that for an organization man of this kind the traditional Protestant ethic is becoming too distant from reality to provide an acceptable creed. The Protestant ethic is summed up by Whyte as the system of beliefs in the virtues of thrift, hard work and independence, and in the sacredness of property and the enervating effect of security. It extols free competition between individuals in the struggle for wealth and success. But to Whyte life is no longer like this, if it ever was. To him 'that upward path toward the rainbow of achievement leads smack through the conference room'. The younger generation of management have begun to recognize themselves as bureaucrats, even if they cannot face the word itself and prefer to describe themselves as administrators.

Such people need a different faith to give meaning to what they do, and Whyte finds in American society a gradually emerging body of thought to meet the need. He calls it the *social ethic*. This ethic provides the moral justification for the pressures of society against the individual. It holds that the individual is meaningless by himself, but that by being absorbed into the group he can create a whole that is greater than the sum of its parts. There should be no conflicts between man and society; any that occur are misunderstandings which can be prevented by better human relations.

There are three major propositions in the social ethic: *scientism, belongingness* and *togetherness*. Scientism, as Whyte dubs it, is the belief that a science of man can be created in the same way as the physical sciences were developed. If only there were enough time and money, the conditions apposite to good group dynamics or to personal adjustment to social situations or any other desired human response could be discovered. Believers in scientism (who are not to be confused with social scientists) could then generate the belongingness and togetherness which they seek for all. The ultimate need of man, it is thought, is to belong to a group, to harmonize himself with a group. But man needs togetherness in belonging. He wants not merely to be a part of The Organization but to immerse himself in it together with other people, in smaller groups around the conference table, in the seminar, the discussion group, the project team and so on.

Whyte traces the career cycle of organization man as, guided by his social ethic, he gives himself up to The Organization. The influence of The Organization has extended into college curricula, and by the time students are looking for their first job they have already turned their backs on the Protestant ethic. They look for a life of calm and order, offering success but not too much success, money but not too much, advancement but not too far. The Organization attempts to recruit for itself those who will fit in, those who will get along well with others, those who will not have any disturbingly exceptional characteristics. Increasingly it uses the tools of the psychologist: not only the well-tried aptitude and intelligence tests but tests purporting to reveal personality. Whyte challenges the validity of these latter tests, and goes so far as to write an Appendix entitled 'How to Cheat on Personality Tests'. To obtain a safe personality score, you should try to answer as if you were like everybody else is supposed to be.

Once recruited, the training of the potential manager emphasizes not his own work but the exploitation of human relations techniques to manage the work of others. The successful trainee is not the one who competes successfully with the others but the one who cooperates more than the others cooperate. What of the loss of individualism in group life? Young men today, says Whyte, regard this aspect of the large organization as a positive boon. Their ideal is 'the well-rounded man'. Such a man has time for family and hobbies. He is good on the job but not too zealous or over-involved in it: overwork may have been necessary in the past but now The Organization looks for 'the full man'. In particular, this is the image held by the personnel manager and the business school.

The same tendencies Whyte also sees in scientific and academic institutions. The idea of the lone genius is being displaced by that of the group-conscious research team. There is a steady increase in the proportion of scientific papers by several authors compared with those by a single author.

Though Whyte is stating a case against too great a belief in the social ethic, he realistically points out that it may never be applied as absolutely as it is preached, any more than was the Protestant ethic. Even so, the social ethic may delude the individual that his interests are being cared for when The Organization is really following its own ends. Guided by it, The Organization may suppress individual imagination, and may cling to a mediocre consensus. People may become skilful in getting along with one another yet fail to ask why they should get along; may strive for adjustment, but fail to ask what they are adjusting. It is Whyte's contention that organization man must fight The Organization, and accept conflict between himself and society.

However, for some few in The Organization who start to go ahead of their contemporaries there comes a realization that they have committed themselves: that they must go on alone to higher executive positions, that their home lives will be shortened and their wives less and less interested in the struggle. Such men find themselves working fifty- and sixty-hour weeks; taking work home; spending weekends at conferences. They have no time for anything else. More than this, their work is their self-expression and they do not want anything else. They discover that the man on his way to the top cannot be 'well-rounded'. The dream of a comfortable contentment just short of the top is shattered, and they talk of the treadmill, the merry-go-round, and the rat race, 'words that convey an absence of tangible goals but plenty of activity to get there'.

So the executive contains within himself the conflict between the old Protestant ethic and the new social ethic. The man who goes ahead does so to control his own destiny; yet in The Organization he must be controlled *and* look as if he likes it. Even though he wants to be dominant, he must applaud permissive management. He has risen by being a good team player but now more and more he sees the other side – the frustration of the committee, the boredom of being sociable. Here is the executive's neurosis.

Bibliography

Whyte, W. H., *The Organization Man,* New York: John Day, 1941.

John Kenneth Galbraith

J. K. Galbraith was born in Canada, but has lived most of his life in the USA. He is an economist who has spent his academic years at Harvard University. He was a supporter of John Kennedy and during the Kennedy administration served as US Ambassador to India. Galbraith has long believed in the necessity of popularizing the ideas of economics, and his books are as much aimed at the layman as the professional economist.

His underlying thesis in all his work is that American capitalism has changed its nature over the past fifty years and, as a result, traditional economic theories no longer apply. Classical economic theory rests on the proposition that the behaviour of buyers and sellers is regulated by the market, through which the stimulant of competition is provided. Economic power is denied to any one person or firm because of price competition. But this system depends on a large number of producers of a good or service, none of whom is in a position to dominate the market; conversely it depends on large numbers of buyers, who individually cannot affect the market. Yet this is demonstrably not the situation in modern industrial economies. Instead there is a process by which the typical industry passes from an initial stage of many firms competing, to a situation of a few large firms only, i.e. what economists refer to as oligopoly.

Thus, the most important task facing modern economic theory is to analyse the place of the large corporation in the economy, and to discover what, if any, new regulatory agencies have replaced the marketplace. If the balanced power of the competitive system no longer applies, does the large corporation wield unchecked power? In *American Capitalism*, Galbraith suggests that there is a situation of countervailing power. The concentration of industrial enterprise, on which everyone agrees, produces the giant corporations which might possibly produce huge agglomerations of power both in economic and political terms. But this process brings into existence strong buyers as well as strong sellers. This is something that tends to be forgotten when the supposed 'evils' of oligopology are discussed. An example of such countervailing power is seen in the development of large retail trading chains, such as Marks & Spencer and the Co-Operative Movement, who from their importance as buyers of goods are able to offset the oligopoly power of the producers or sellers of shirts, dresses, etc. Similarly, in the labour market there is the power of the union countervailing that of the employers' association. Thus, the situation is one of giants standing off against each other. Much of the increasing intervention in the economy by the state comes from the need to develop sources of countervailing power in the economy. A recent phenomenon in the USA and Britain which fits the theory is the development of vocal consumers' associations.

So, the competitive marketplace as regulator is replaced, due to the differences between the capitalistic system of today and that of fifty years ago. And such a system has its efficiencies. It is the large oligopolies which can best incur the cost of research. However, Galbraith himself points out that this system of countervailing power really only works where there is limited demand, so that the buyer has some leeway *vis-à-vis* the seller. In the context of unlimited demand the balance of power shifts decisively to the seller, the large corporation. And in *The Affluent Society* and *The New Industrial State* he develops the idea of control of the market by the corporation, where a situation of unlimited demand is 'manufactured'.

Again the starting idea is the rise of the large-scale corporation and separation of ownership from control and the results of this for a competitive market system (see Burnham, p. 211). Control of the market becomes increasingly important for the well-being of the organization because of the use of more and more sophisticated technology. The organization faces a set of technological imperatives (technology being the systematic application of scientific or other organized knowledge to practical tasks). For Galbraith there are six imperatives deriving from increased technological sophistication which have important implications for the relationship of the organization to other organizations, to the consumer, and to the state.

First, the time-span between thinking of a new product and actually producing it is getting greater and greater. An example is the lead time between the initial idea for a car and its arrival on the market. Secondly, the amount of capital that is committed to production increases; more investment is required. Thirdly, once time and money have been committed there is a great deal of inflexibility; it becomes very difficult to back out. Fourthly, the use of advanced technology requires special sorts of manpower and we have the rise of the engineer, the applied scientist, the importance of technical qualifications. (As with Burnham, Galbraith sees this 'technostructure' becoming the important source of decision-making.) Fifthly, organizations become more complex, with an increasing need for the control and coordination of the specialists. Sixthly, all these imperatives together produce the need for planning.

Thus, societies require large corporations (which Galbraith names The Industrial System, the dominant feature of the New Industrial State) properly to acquire the benefits of new technology. But it is obvious that the imperatives outlined above involve the organization in situations of risk. There are always the famous cases of the Ford Edsel and the Rolls-Royce aero-engines as salutory reminders of what can happen when planning fails. It is only the large business organization which can find the necessary capital and employ the necessary skills to use sophisticated technology, but it still needs help in dealing with this, and with the risks involved.

Organizational planning does not just mean making sure that the right materials get to the right place at the right time, internally. It also means that suppliers are reliable, producing goods, components, etc., as needed, and that the buyers are there when needed. As a result, to quote Galbraith: 'Much of what the firm regards as planning consists in minimizing or getting rid of market influences.' To deal with the uncertainties involved, and thus minimize the risks facing the organization, planning is required to *replace the market*. Control of the market can be done in two ways: either by direct control of the consumer, making him dependent in some way on the corporation, or by having a single customer – a guaranteed market. Both of these options involve increasing state intervention, another illustration of the changing nature of contemporary capitalism.

Direct control of the consumer can take place in a variety of ways. One of the most important is the use of advertising. This is a direct attempt to influence the demand for a product and also to create a psychological dependence on the part of the consumer. Under conditions of affluence a situation of unlimited demand can be created with the corporation controlling the needs and aspirations of the consumer rather than vice versa. In the USA the accepted view of a desirable automobile is the current model as styled in and by Detroit. A further possibility is the control of the market by size domination, a movement towards monopoly. This can be helped along by vertical integration and the use of contracts to tie buyers and sellers together, stabilizing the existence of both. The state is important in that it now carries the responsibility for regulating the level of demand in the economy, stabilizing wages and prices.

Having a single customer guaranteed market becomes extremely important for those organizations having especially advanced, expensive technologies. In particular what happens is that the state becomes the customer and the idea of a market starts to disappear altogether. The state is in effect underwriting the cost of investment, and the line between the 'private' corporation and the state begins to disappear. This situation is typical of the aerospace industry, where research, development and production are commissioned by the government. An organization such as Lockheed sells more than three-quarters of its production to the government.

With the need to control demand, and the role of the state in this process, there is a tendency for the corporation to become a part of the administrative arm of the state. The management of demand becomes a vast, rapidly growing industry in which the public sector is increasingly important through its control of the wage-price spiral, its control of personal and corporate income tax, its regulation of aggregate demand, and its own role as a consumer. Also the state is responsible for producing the qualified manpower (the technostructure) on which the corporation is dependent, through its financing of education.

The net result is an increasing similarity between all mature industrial societies in terms of the design of organizations and the planning mechanisms used. The heavy requirements of capital, sophisticated technology and elaborate organization, which need planning to replace the market, lead to the dominance of the large corporation. And such corporations are dependent on the state. As Galbraith summarizes his position: 'Given the decision to have modern industry (in any country), much of what happens is inevitable and the same.'

Bibliography

Galbraith, J. K., The Affluent Society, New York: Houghton Mifflin, 1958.
Galbraith, J. K., *American Capitalism,* Houghton Mifflin, 1962.
Galbraith, J. K., *The New Industrial State,* Houghton Mifflin, 1967.
Galbraith, J. K., *The Age of Uncertainty,* Houghton Mifflin, 1977.

E. Fritz Schumacher

Born in Germany, Fritz Schumacher (1911–1977) went to Britain in 1930 to study economics at New College, Oxford, and from there to Columbia University, New York. He later turned from the academic life to business, farming, and journalism. His public service for Britain included serving from 1946 to 1950 as Economic Adviser to the British Control Commission in Germany, and from 1950 to 1970 as Economic Adviser to the National Coal Board. He was Founder and Chairman of the Intermediate Technology Development Group Ltd, President of the Soil Association (an organic farming organization), and a Director of the Scott-Bader Company.

To Schumacher the belief by economists and industrialists alike that mankind has solved the problem of production is glib nonsense. It is 'solved' only by the industrialized nations consuming resources at a frenetic pace. Production is using up the natural capital of our planet without which it cannot itself continue. Even supposing that there were resources sufficient for all peoples to use energy at the rate at which it is now used in the industrialized nations, if they did so the world level of thermal and nuclear pollution would be intolerable.

We must begin to evolve a new life-style with methods of production and of consumption that are designed for permanence, based on biologically sound agriculture and on 'non-violent technology' which does not do violence to resources or to people. We need 'technology with a human face'.

The fragmentary view given by Western economics is too narrow to see this. Its exclusive focus on readily quantifiable goods ignores the 'free goods' from which these derive. An activity can be economic even though it destroys the environment, whilst a competing activity which conserves the environment will be made to appear more costly and therefore uneconomic.

Even work itself is seen as labour, as a cost, as a disutility, as a sacrifice of leisure. It is not seen as a desirable activity in which individuals use their faculties of brain and hand, join others in a common task, and find purpose in bringing forth needed goods and services. Virtually all production has been turned by large-scale technology into an inhuman chore where the work of brain and of hand are separated, despite the needs of a human being for both.

Technology and the organization making use of technology ought to fit the resources of our planet and the needs of man. They must be of an appropriate scale. 'Man is small, and, therefore, small is beautiful. To go for giantism is to go for self-destruction.'

From this critique stems Schumacher's advocacy of 'intermediate technology' and organization for the third world, and 'smallness within bigness' for the organizations of the industrialized world.

Intermediate technology should replace the 'technology of giantism'. The trend towards ever-greater size of production equipment, and of larger organizations to run it at ever-higher speeds, is the opposite of progress. Third world poverty is a problem of two million villages to which such technologies and organizations are wholly unsuited. They result in incongruous and costly projects. A textile mill in Africa is filled with highly automated machinery to 'eliminate the human factor' even though people are idle, and even though its standards demand fibres of a length not grown locally so that its raw materials must be imported. A soap factory produces luxury soap by such sensitive processes that only very refined materials can be used, which are imported at high prices whilst local materials are exported at low prices. Examples of such inaptness abound.

As Gandhi said, the poor of the world cannot be helped by mass production but only by production by the masses. So the best of modern knowledge should be applied to designing technology at a level which is conducive to decentralized moderate-scale production that is 'gentle', not violent, in its use of scarce resources, and serves the human being rather than him serving it. This intermediate technology should be a means for people to help themselves, making what their countries need rather than sophisticated products usable only by the rich populations of the industrialized world. It should enable them to work in a way fitting for them. Their first need is for work that brings in some reward, however small; not until they experience some value in their time and effort can they become interested in making it more valuable.

Schumacher argues that the smallest-scale technology and organization suitable for the purpose should be used. He puts forward four propositions:

1. Workplaces should be created where people live now, not in the metropolitan areas to which they then migrate.
2. These workplaces should be cheap enough to be created in large numbers without calling for unattainable levels of capital formation and imports.
3. Production methods should be sufficiently simple to minimize demands for high skills either in production or in organization.
4. Production should be mainly from local materials and for local use.

The intermediate level of technology may be symbolized in monetary terms. Suppose that the indigenous technology of a typical developing country is called a £1-technology, and that of developed countries is called a £1000-technology, then intermediate technology is a £100-technology.

It has been objected that using such a technology is deliberately denying people the chance to be as productive as possible. Productivity should not be deliberately held down in order to limit the amount of capital per worker. People should not be prevented from increasing their wealth as quickly as possible by the latest methods. Schumacher's rejoinder is that this overlooks the real situation, and the capabilities and needs of the people themselves. It is a mistake to assume that sophisticated equipment in an unsuitable situation will be efficient at the level projected for it in an industrialized society. Not only are the technical and administrative skills not available, but industrial estates all over the third world stand half idle because the assumed supporting communications, transport, distribution network and imported materials and components are not in fact there.

Whilst intermediate technology in the third world would require the organizing of people in small units, the giant organizations of the industrialized world cannot simply be abolished. Some goods can only be produced on a large scale. So what can be done about these giants? The fundamental task is to achieve *smallness within bigness*.

Bigness ensues from the constant mergers and takeovers in

private industry, and from nationalization in the public sector, especially in the socialist countries. Individuals come to feel mere cogs in vast machines. Kafka's nightmarish novel, *The Castle*, depicts the devastating effects of remote control on an individual who gropes within the system to find what is what and who is who, perpetually mystified and confused. No one likes large organizations, yet Parkinsonian bureaucracies continue to grow.

What organizations need are both the orderliness of *order* and the disorderliness of creative *freedom*. Large organizations are pulled to and fro by these two needs, and in consequence go through alternating phases of centralizing and decentralizing as they give priority first to the one and then to the other. Unfortunately, administrative demands tend to bias them towards orderliness and centralization at the expense of the disorderly decentralization which allows scope for entrepreneurial innovation. Perhaps what is needed is neither centralization nor decentralization but 'the-one-and-the-other-at-the-same-time', both together.

This leads Schumacher to formulate five principles for running large-scale organizations, which are essentially aimed at devolving them into relatively autonomous profit centres.

First is the *Principle of Subsidiarity*, or the Principle of Subsidiary Function. A higher level in an organization should never do what a lower level can do. So a large organization will consist of many semi-autonomous units. From an administrator's point of view this will appear untidy compared to a clear-cut monolith, but the centre will actually gain in authority and effectiveness because of the loyalty engendered in the lower units (see also Tannenbaum, p. 78).

Accountability of the subsidiary units to the centre requires the application of the second principle, the *Principle of Vindication*. Other than in exceptional cases, the subsidiary unit should be defended against reproach and upheld: and it should be assessed on the minimum number of criteria of accountability so that it knows clearly whether or not it is performing satisfactorily. In a commercial organization there would ideally be only one criterion, profitability. Numerous criteria mean that fault can always be found on one item or another, which stifles initiative.

Hence the third principle, the *Principle of Identification*. It must be possible for each unit to identify clearly its cumulative success or failure by having not only a separate profit and loss account but a separate balance sheet of assets. The effect of its own efforts on its own economic substance is then visible.

Fourthly, the *Principle of Motivation* calls for a positive approach to work. If all efforts are devoted only to doing away with work by automation and computerization, it comes to be regarded as something to be got rid of. It becomes a devalued activity which people put up with because no other way has been found of doing it. They work just for the pay.

Finally there is the *Principle of the Middle Axiom* which the centre should follow if it wants to get things done. For if it tries to get things done by exhortation, nothing will happen. If it tries to get things done by issuing detailed instructions, these may be erroneous because they are not from the people closely in touch with the actual job. What is required is something in between, a middle axiom. This is an axiom because it is sufficiently self-evident to command consent, and also is clear enough for others to know what to do.

The incomprehensibility of large organizations to those in them is exacerbated by their forms of ownership. In small-scale enterprise, private ownership is 'natural, fruitful, and just', in Schumacher's view. But in medium-scale enterprise, private ownership begins to lose its function. Its contribution begins to disappear. Whilst in large-scale enterprise, private ownership 'is a fiction for the purpose of enabling functionless owners to live parasitically on the labour of others'. It 'distorts all relationships within the enterprise'.

Nationalization is a purely negative extinguishing of private rights without substituting anything positive. Schumacher describes one alternative exemplified by the Scott-Bader Commonwealth with which he himself became connected. In this polymer chemistry firm, private ownership was replaced by Commonwealth ownership. All employees are members of the Commonwealth which as a collectivity, without individual ownership rights, owns Scott-Bader Co. Ltd.

This kind of solution would be applicable only in small to medium size organizations. For larger organizations, Schumacher makes radical suggestions as to how a public share in the equity could be achieved. He proposes that instead of profits being taxed, the public be issued with equity shares. In harmony with his views on the local character of industries that use intermediate technology, he proposes that these shares be held locally in the district where the enterprise is located. One way for this to be done would be to vest the shares in Social Councils composed of members from local trade unions, local professional associations and local residents.

To Schumacher, small is beautiful because it is the way to humane efficiency in the organizations of our time.

Bibliography

Schumacher, E. F., *Small is Beautiful: A Study of Economics as if People Mattered,* State Mutual Book, 1981.
McRobie, G., *Small is Possible,* Harper & Row, 1981.

Name Index

Subject Index